Notes On Graphic Design And Visual Communication

Gregg Berryman

Revised Edition

Crisp Publications, Inc.
95 First Street
Los Altos, California 94022

Library of Congress Cataloging in Publication Data

Berryman, Gregg.
    Notes on graphic design and visual communication.

    Cover title.
    1. Graphic arts.   2. Visual perception.
I. Title.
NC997.B43   1984   741.6   83-24902

ISBN 1-56052-044-2
Revised Edition

10 9 8 7 6 5

INTRODUCTION

■ THIS COLLECTION OF NOTES ON GRAPHIC DESIGN IS BASED ON OVER FIFTEEN YEARS EXPERIENCE TEACHING GRAPHIC DESIGN CONCEPTS TO MANY HUNDREDS OF BEGINNING STUDENTS AT THE UNIVERSITY LEVEL. GRASPING THE FUNDAMENTAL TECHNIQUES, CONCEPTS AND PRINCIPLES OF VISUAL COMMUNICATION IS ABSOLUTELY CRITICAL, WHETHER YOUR PERSONAL GOAL IS VISUAL LITERACY OR PROFESSIONAL PRACTICE IN DESIGN. THE FOUNDATION IS THE MOST IMPORTANT PART OF THE DESIGN EDUCATION PROCESS AND MUST BE SOLID. GOOD STRONG BASICS HELP THE DESIGNER DEVELOP A PROBLEM SOLVING APPROACH BASED ON HISTORICAL AWARENESS AND VISUAL INTELLIGENCE. THE ONLY ALTERNATIVE IS A KIND OF VISUAL NAIVETY, AT BEST SHALLOW AND AT ITS WORST ABSOLUTELY DANGEROUS. GRAPHIC DESIGN CAN ILL AFFORD AMATEURS.

■ CONSIDERABLE PROFESSIONAL PRACTICE IN THE FIELD OF GRAPHIC DESIGN HAS TEMPERED MY PERSONAL VIEW OF THE DESIGN PROCESS. TWO FORCES ARE IN CONSTANT OPPOSITION. THESE NEED TO BE CAREFULLY CULTIVATED, TAMED, AND BROUGHT INTO A DELICATE HARMONY. SELF-EXPRESSION OR PERSONAL CREATIVITY MUST BE BALANCED BY THE CONSTANT NEED TO SATISFY AN AUDIENCE IN A LOGICAL RATIONAL MANNER WITHIN ECONOMIC LIMITS. IF THE FORCES CAN BE MADE COMPLEMENTARY, THE DESIGN PROCESS CAN FLOW AND EFFECTIVE DESIGN CAN RESULT. DESIGN IS NOT ART BUT IS A CREATIVE PURSUIT AND CAN BRING EQUAL SATISFACTION.

■ THESE NOTES HAVE BEEN ASSEMBLED TO BRING TOGETHER IN A SINGLE SOURCE, CAREFULLY TESTED CONCEPTS. SUPPORTED BY SELECTED VISUAL EXAMPLES AND SPECIFIC REFERENCE READING, THESE CONCEPTS CAN HELP LAUNCH SERIOUS DESIGN STUDY. THE LAYOUT PLAN HAS BEEN TO KEEP RELATED NOTES TOGETHER IN SPREADS. HAND LETTERING WAS CHOSEN RATHER THAN TYPESETTING TO EXPLAIN DESIGN CONCEPTS. LETTERING IS PERSONAL AND IS INTENDED TO HELP REMOVE SOME OF THE "MYSTERY" OF DESIGN AS SEEN BY MANY BEGINNING STUDENTS. AN ATTEMPT HAS BEEN MADE TO SIMPLIFY THE LANGUAGE OF DESIGN, A CONSTANT AND VERY DIFFICULT PROBLEM. YOUR FEEDBACK AND SUGGESTIONS ARE WELCOME. *Gregg Berryman*

CONTENTS

DESIGN

de·sign (di-zīn′), *v.t.* [OFr. *designer*; L. *designare*, to mark out, define; *de-*, out, from + *signare*, to mark < *signum*, a mark, sign]. 1. to plan; make preliminary sketches of; sketch a pattern or outline for. 2. to form (plans, etc.) in the mind; contrive. 3. to plan to do; purpose; intend. 4. to intend or set apart for some purpose. *v.i.* 1. to make designs. 2. to make original plans, sketches, patterns, etc.: as, she *designs* for a coat manufacturer. *n.* [Fr. *dessein*; It. *disegno* < *disegnare*; L. *designare*], 1. a plan; scheme; project. 2. purpose; intention; aim. 3. a thing planned for or outcome aimed at. 4. a working out by plan: as, do we find a *design* in history? 5. *pl.* a secret or sinister scheme (often with *on* or *upon*): as, he has *designs* on her property. 6. a plan or sketch to work from; pattern: as, a *design* for a house. 7. the art of making designs or patterns. 8. the arrangement of parts, details, form, color, etc., especially so as to produce a complete and artistic unit; artistic invention: as, the *design* of a rug. 9. a finished artistic work. —*SYN.* see **intend, plan.**

• DICTIONARY DEFINITIONS FROM WEBSTER'S NEW WORLD DICTIONARY, COLLEGE ED.

THE DESIGN NECESSITY

FROM THE FIRST FEDERAL DESIGN ASSEMBLY AUTHORED BY: CHERMAYEFF, WURMAN, CAPLAN AND BRADFORD

■ DESIGN MAY BE CONSIDERED AS AN INSTRUMENT OF ORGANIZATION, A MEDIUM FOR PERSUASION, A MEANS OF RELATING OBJECTS TO PEOPLE, AND A METHOD FOR IMPROVING SAFETY AND EFFICIENCY.

■ DESIGN MUST PERFORM IN RESPONSE TO HUMAN NEEDS. DESIGN PERFORMANCE SHOULD BE DEMONSTRABLE OR MEASURABLE.

● THERE ARE SOUND, PROVEN CRITERIA FOR JUDGING DESIGN EFFECTIVENESS.

● DESIGN IS AN URGENT REQUIREMENT, NOT A COSMETIC ADDITION. DESIGN IS ESSENTIAL TO SURVIVAL (RESOURCE PLANNING).

● EFFECTIVE DESIGN CAN SAVE MONEY BY REDUCING THE COST OF LABOR, MATERIALS AND PRODUCTION.

● DESIGN CAN SAVE TIME BY PRESENTING INFORMATION MORE CLEARLY.

● DESIGN ENHANCES COMMUNICATION. IT HELPS MORE PEOPLE TO UNDERSTAND A GIVEN MESSAGE. DESIGN HELPS ACCELERATE LEARNING.

● DESIGN SIMPLIFIES USE, MANUFACTURE, AND REPAIR. DESIGN HELPS MACHINES AND TOOLS FIT THE HUMAN BODY.

THE ABSENCE OF DESIGN IS A HAZARDOUS KIND OF DESIGN. NOT TO DESIGN IS TO SUFFER DESIGN BY DEFAULT. WE CANNOT AFFORD TO HAVE GRAPHICS, PRODUCTS, AND ARCHITECTURE "JUST HAPPEN!"

■ EVERYONE IS A DESIGNER TO A CERTAIN EXTENT. YOU ARE ALSO. WHETHER YOU ARE CHOOSING A COLOR FOR YOUR HOUSE OR ROOM, OR BUYING CLOTHES OR CUSTOMIZING AN AUTOMOBILE, THE CHOICES YOU MAKE ARE DESIGN DECISIONS.

■ DESIGN IS FINDING THE BEST SOLUTION TO A PROBLEM WITHIN THE LIMITATIONS OF THE PROBLEM (NEEDS, COST, TIME).

■ DESIGN DIFFERS FROM MATHEMATICS OR CHEMISTRY IN THAT MORE THAN A SINGLE SOLUTION EXISTS FOR EACH PROBLEM. WE CALL THESE ALTERNATE SOLUTIONS. DESIGNERS ATTEMPT TO FIND THE OPTIMUM OR "BEST" OF THE ALTERNATIVE SOLUTIONS AND BRING IT INTO USE.

1 GRAPHIC DESIGN — DESIGNS PEOPLE READ: BOOKS, MAGAZINES, ADS, PACKAGES, SIGNS, FILM AND TELEVISION TITLES, POSTERS, BROCHURES, EXHIBITS.

2 PRODUCT DESIGN — THINGS PEOPLE USE: TOOLS, MACHINES, VEHICLES, INSTRUMENTS, CONTROLS, STRUCTURES.

3 ENVIRONMENTAL DESIGN — WHERE PEOPLE LIVE: INTERIORS, STRUCTURES, BUILDINGS, HOMES, GARDENS, PARKS, CITIES.

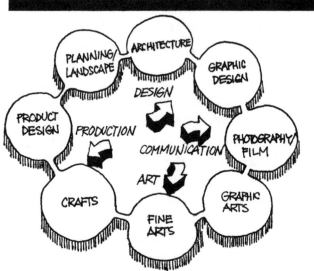

GRAPHIC DESIGN

■GRAPHIC DESIGNERS ARE DESIGN GENERALISTS CONCERNED WITH INFORMATION TO BE READ. THEY ARE INVOLVED WITH AFFECTING AN AUDIENCE. THEY TRY TO GET MOST OF THE PEOPLE IN A TARGET GROUP TO RESPOND POSITIVELY TO A VISUAL MESSAGE.

■GRAPHIC DESIGNERS USE TYPOGRAPHY, SYMBOLISM, ILLUSTRATION AND PHOTOGRAPHY TO COMMUNICATE VISUALLY. OFTEN A COMBINATION OF THESE TECHNIQUES IS EFFECTIVE.

■GRAPHIC DESIGNERS WORK FOR CORPORATIONS, INSTITUTIONS (HOSPITALS, UNIVERSITIES) AND GOVERNMENTS. THEY WORK EITHER IN-HOUSE FOR ONE ORGANIZATION OR AS CONSULTANTS FOR A NUMBER OF DIFFERENT CLIENTS.

■GRAPHIC DESIGNERS ATTEMPT TO ACHIEVE VISUAL SOLUTIONS THAT ARE FUNCTIONAL, ELEGANT, APPROPRIATE, SIMPLE, AND ECONOMICAL. THEY SOLVE PROBLEMS THAT RANGE FROM THE SIMPLICITY OF A SALES POSTER TO THE COMPLEXITY OF A SIGN SYSTEM FOR AN INTERNATIONAL AIRPORT.

GRAPHIC DESIGN IS <u>NOT</u> ART. THE FINE ARTIST HAS AN AUDIENCE OF ONLY ONE (HERSELF OR HIMSELF). THE GRAPHIC DESIGNER DEALS WITH A MASS AUDIENCE OF SOMETIMES MILLIONS. <u>INTENT</u> IS DIFFERENT. OFTEN GRAPHIC DESIGN LOOKS LIKE ART (AND VISE VERSA). MATERIALS AND TECHNIQUES ARE SIMILAR. BOTH ARTIST AND DESIGNER SOLVE VISUAL PROBLEMS. THE ARTIST SATISFIES SELF WHILE THE DESIGNER MUST MOVE GROUPS OF PEOPLE TO ATTEND AN EVENT FOLLOW A SIGN, UNDERSTAND A MAP, LEARN A SCIENTIFIC PRINCIPLE OR BUY A PRODUCT.

GRAPHIC DESIGNERS WORK ON THE FOLLOWING:

SYMBOLS	BROCHURES	FILM TITLES
LOGOS	FORMS	ANNUAL REPORTS
BOOKS	LETTERHEADS	BUSINESS CARDS
MAGAZINES	POSTERS	RECORD JACKETS
NEWSPAPERS	MAPS	CALENDARS
PACKAGES	DIRECTORIES	CHARTS/GRAPHS
SIGN SYSTEMS	BILLBOARDS	VEHICLE IDENTITY
ADS	PROMOTIONS	SUPERGRAPHICS
EXHIBITS	GAMES	COMPUTER GRAPHICS
CATALOGUES	TV GRAPHICS	ETC.

■GRAPHIC DESIGNERS COMMUNICATE AND EXPRESS THEMSELVES IN FOUR DISTINCT WAYS. VERY FEW MASTER ALL FOUR, BUT ALL NEED TO HAVE A WORKING KNOWLEDGE OF TYPOGRAPHY, SYMBOLISM, ILLUSTRATION, AND PHOTOGRAPHY/FILM. DESIGNERS' SPECIALTIES:

●PHOTOGRAPHY/FILM
SAUL BASS
JAY MAISEL
LOU DORFSMAN
MORTON GOLDSHALL
ART KANE

●ILLUSTRATION
MARK ENGLISH
MILTON GLASER
DON WELLER
BERNIE FUCHS
HEATHER COOPER
GENE HOFFMAN

●SYMBOLISM
PAUL RAND
ROD DYER
JOE SELAME
HARRY MURPHY
PRIMO ANGELI
TOM GEISMAR

●TYPOGRAPHY
BILL BONNELL
HERB LUBALIN
TOM CARNASE
BEN ROSEN
W. WEINGART
MO LEBOWITZ

■GRAPHIC DESIGNERS MUST BE FAMILIAR WITH ALL THE TECHNIQUES OF VISUAL CREATION. IF THEY CANNOT TAKE A SPECIAL PHOTO THEY MUST KNOW WHO TO HIRE, HOW TO ART DIRECT THE PHOTO SESSION, AND HOW TO CHOOSE THE BEST TRANSPARENCY OR PRINT FOR REPRODUCTION. THEY KNOW HOW TO BUY EFFECTIVE ILLUSTRATION AND USE IT PROPERLY. THE GRAPHIC DESIGNER NEEDS TO KNOW BASIC MARKETING CONCEPTS AND HOW THEY AFFECT VISUAL IMAGERY. IT IS NECESSARY FOR THE DESIGNER TO HAVE EXCELLENT EYE-HAND COORDINATION AND AN ABILITY TO WORK NEATLY WITH PRECISION.

■A THOROUGH UNDERSTANDING OF REPRODUCTION PROCESSES ENABLES THE DESIGNER TO ASSEMBLE A JOB, SHEPHERD IT THROUGH PRINTING, AND DELIVER IT ON TIME WITH QUALITY CONTROL. THE MOST EFFECTIVE DESIGNERS HAVE FRESH, INNOVATIVE IDEAS, AND A CONCERN FOR DETAIL THAT ALLOWS THEIR IDEAS TO FLOURISH.

■DESIGNERS NEED TO HAVE "PEOPLE SKILLS" TO DEAL WITH CLIENTS, SUPPLIERS, SUBCONTRACTORS, BANKERS, LAWYERS, PRINTERS, AND ASSOCIATES.

ROOTS

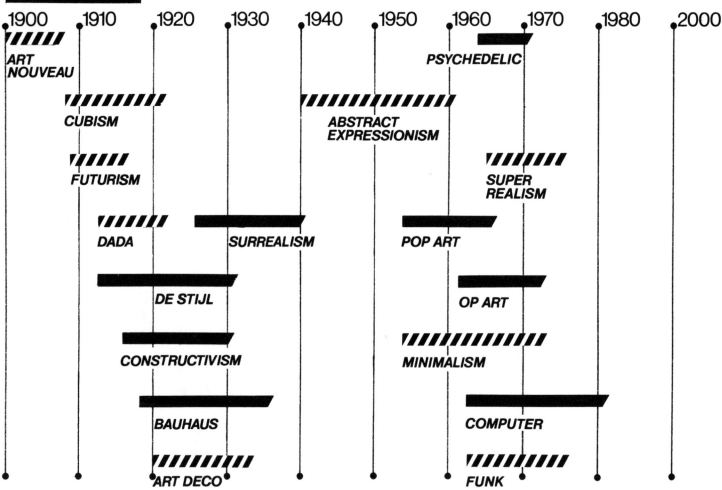

| 1900 | 1910 | 1920 | 1930 | 1940 | 1950 | 1960 | 1970 | 1980 | 2000 |

ART NOUVEAU

PSYCHEDELIC

CUBISM

ABSTRACT EXPRESSIONISM

FUTURISM

SUPER REALISM

DADA   SURREALISM   POP ART

DE STIJL   OP ART

CONSTRUCTIVISM   MINIMALISM

BAUHAUS   COMPUTER

ART DECO   FUNK

▬▬ BOLD LINES SHOW MOVEMENTS MOST IMPORTANT TO GRAPHIC DESIGN

MOVEMENT
STYLE

SCHOOL
CLASS

INDIVIDUAL
ARTISTS

THIS DIAGRAM INDICATES HOW MOST ART MOVEMENTS GROW FROM THE WORK OF INDIVIDUAL ARTISTS.

GRAPHIC DESIGN ORIGINS · PROFESSIONAL GRAPHIC DESIGN BEGAN IN EUROPE. VALID DESIGN EDUCATION BEGAN IN GERMANY AT THE BAUHAUS IN THE 1920'S. GRAPHIC DESIGN EDUCATION BEGAN IN THE U.S. AFTER WW2. MANY EARLY DESIGNERS WERE TRAINED IN FINE ARTS, STAGE DESIGN, ARCHITECTURE, OR PHOTOGRAPHY. FOR ALL ITS IMPACT ON COMMUNICATION, GRAPHIC DESIGN IS A YOUNG FIELD.

■AS A RULE FINE ARTS (SPECIFICALLY PAINTING) HAS PRECEDED IN VISUAL FORM [STYLE] WHAT HAS HAPPENED IN GRAPHIC DESIGN. THE ROOTS OF GRAPHIC DESIGN ARE IN THE GREAT FINE ARTS TRADITIONS AND MOVEMENTS. TWO NOTABLE EXCEPTIONS ARE POP ART AND COMPUTER ART WHERE EXISTING GRAPHICS (PACKAGES, BILLBOARDS, AND DRAFTING IMAGES) INFLUENCED PAINTING MOVEMENTS.

ABOUT STYLE · BE CAREFUL TO KEEP STYLE IN ITS HISTORICAL PERSPECTIVE! IMAGES WHICH ARE ONLY FASHIONABLE AND GROW OUT OF THE IMITATION OF A HISTORICAL STYLE LACK INTEGRITY. A VALID VISUAL STYLE IS THE RESULT OF WORKING TOWARD THE LEADING EDGE OF VISUAL COMMUNICATION. THE DEVELOPMENT OF A UNIQUE GRAPHIC STYLE COMES FROM WORKING IN A SERIES OR SEQUENCE AND PUSHING AT VISUAL LIMITS.

ART NOUVEAU • STEERED AWAY FROM IMITATION. ▮▮▮▮▮▮ INSPIRATION DERIVED FROM FLOWING TWISTING SHAPES OF PLANTS, VINES, LEAVES, FLOWERS. EMPHASIS ON SURFACE DECORATION, ORNAMENT. ORIGIN OF POSTER AS AN ART FORM. ILLUSTRATIONS, LETTERFORMS, ORNAMENT LAUNCHED FUTURE GRAPHIC IDEAS. BEARDSLEY, TOULOUSE-LAUTREC.

CUBISM • TOTAL BREAK WITH IMAGE PRESENTATION. ▮▮▮▮ FRAGMENTATION, MULTIPLE VIEWPOINTS, COLLAGE, ASSEMBLAGE, LETTERFORMS AS VISUAL ELEMENTS. PICASSO, BRAQUE.

FUTURISM • INTEGRATION OF CUBISM AND MOTION. ▮▮▮▮ MACHINE ELEMENTS AND KINEMATICS AS DESIGN ELEMENTS. CONVERSION OF TIME INTO VISUAL FORM MUCH LIKE STROBE PHOTOGRAPHY. DUCHAMP, BOCCIONI.

DADA • ASKED "WHAT IS ART?" BROADENED IDEAS ▮▮▮ OF WHAT ART COULD BE. USED HUMOR, METAMORPHOSIS, AND SHOCK VALUE AS COMMUNICATION ELEMENTS. TYPOGRAPHIC EXPERIMENTATION. DUCHAMP, MAN-RAY.

SURREALISM • ILLUSTRATIVE IMAGES DERIVED ▮▮▮▮ FROM THE UNCONSCIOUS. VISUAL FORMS FROM DREAMS, HEAVY INFLUENCE OF SIGMUND FREUD. MYSTERIOUS ILLUSTRATIONS AND PHOTOGRAPHS. CLOSE CONTINUATION OF DADA. DALI, MAGRITTE, ESCHER.

CONSTRUCTIVISM • COMBINATION OF WORDS AND ▮▮▮▮▮ IMAGES AS SIMULTANEOUS VISUAL EXPERIENCE. PHOTOGRAMS, PHOTOMONTAGE, SUPERIMPOSITION, VARIABLE FOCUS, CONCRETE TYPOGRAPHY. INNOVATIVE POSTERS AS VEHICLE FOR REVOLUTIONARY COMMUNICATION. ROOTS IN RUSSIAN REVOLUTION. LISSITZKY, MALEVICH.

ART DECO • ORNAMENT AND SURFACE DECORATION ▮▮▮▮ DERIVED FROM CONCEPTS OF ART NOUVEAU BUT USING GEOMETRIC AND MACHINE FORMS. "STREAMLINED" SHAPES, SLICK, SOMETIMES GARISH FINISHES. ORNATE TYPOGRAPHY, BORDERS, CORNERS, DINGBATS. CASSANDRE, HELD.

DE STIJL • PRECISE SPACE DIVISION, SIMPLICITY, BASIC ▮▮▮▮ SHAPES, PRIMARY COLORS, ASYMMETRIC TYPOGRAPHY. RATHER METAPHYSICAL CONCEPTS

RADICALLY ALTERED THE PRINTED PAGE. MOST POWERFUL INFLUENCE ON BAUHAUS, INTERNATIONAL STYLE, AND "SWISS GRAPHICS." MONDRIAN, VAN DOESBURG.

BAUHAUS • PLACE, SCHOOL, IDEAS WHICH DEALT ▮▮▮▮ WITH CREATIVE RELATIONSHIPS OF ART AND TECHNOLOGY. EXTENDED CONSTRUCTIVIST AND DE STIJL IDEAS INTO ALL ASPECTS OF VISUAL COMMUNICATION. INNOVATIVE PHOTOGRAPHY, TYPOGRAPHY. BIRTH OF PROFESSIONAL DESIGN. INTEGRATION OF ARCHITECTURE, PRODUCT DESIGN, FINE ARTS, CRAFTS, THEATER, PHOTOGRAPHY, AND GRAPHIC DESIGN. FOUNDATION OF DESIGN EDUCATION METHODOLOGY. FUNCTIONALISM, COHERENCE, SET DESIGN PHILOSOPHY FOR "INTERNATIONAL STYLE." BAYER, MOHOLY-NAGY, KLEE, ALBERS.

ABSTRACT EXPRESSIONISM • ACTION ART. FORMS FROM ▮▮▮▮▮▮ THE ACT OF MAKING ART. AMERICAN ORIGIN. MYSTERIOUS IMAGERY, FORMS WITHOUT READY REFERENCE. MINOR IMPORTANCE TO GRAPHIC DESIGN. POLLACK, KLINE, DIEBENKORN.

POP ART • FORMS DERIVED FROM GRAPHIC DESIGN— ▮▮▮▮ PACKAGES, SIGNS, BILLBOARDS, ADVERTISING. COMMERCIAL REPRODUCTION TECHNIQUES. EXPANDED SUBJECTS OF ART. JOHNS, RAUSCHENBERG, WARHOL.

OP ART • ILLUSION, COLOR FIELD, OPTICS, GESTALT AS ▮▮▮▮ THE SUBJECT OF ART. STRONG GRIDS, DIAGRAMS. DEALS WITH COLOR PSYCHOLOGY. POSTERS. RILEY, VASARELY.

COMPUTER • ART THROUGH MATHEMATICAL LANGUAGE ▮▮▮▮ BY PROGRAM. LINEAR AND DOT IMAGE MACHINE-MADE ART. ILLUSTRATIVE, TYPOGRAPHIC POTENTIAL. ROOTS IN INDUSTRY. FRANKE, MOHR.

PSYCHEDELIC • SAN FRANCISCO ORIGIN. ROOTS IN ▮▮▮▮▮ DRUGS, PROTEST, ROCK MUSIC. BY "NON-DESIGNERS." INTEGRATED TYPE/ILLUSTRATION/PHOTOS COLOR COMPLEMENTS, POWERFUL POSTERS, INFLUENCED BY ART NOUVEAU. WILSON, MOSCOSO.

MINIMALISM • GREAT ATTENTION TO 2-D AND 3-D ▮▮▮▮▮ SPACE WITH VERY SPARSE DESIGN ELEMENTS. GRIDS, MATHEMATICS. "LESS IS MORE." INTELLECTUAL, ABSTRACT, STRUCTURAL. JUDD, KELLY.

AUDIENCE

■ TO CREATE EFFECTIVE GRAPHICS THE DESIGNER NEEDS TO KNOW IN DEPTH THE PERCEPTUAL CAPABILITIES OF HIS TARGET AUDIENCE. HOW WILL THE INDIVIDUALS IN THE AUDIENCE PERCEIVE INFORMATION? AT A FEW INCHES AS IN A MAGAZINE, AT A FEW FEET AS IN A PACKAGE, ACROSS THE STREET FOR A POSTER, OR AT VERY LONG DISTANCE FOR OUTDOOR ADVERTISING? HOW WELL DOES THE AUDIENCE SEE? CERTAINLY IT WOULD BE FOOLISH TO DESIGN FOR 20/20 VISION.

■ IS PART OF THE AUDIENCE COLOR·BLIND? WILL CERTAIN COLORS AND COLOR COMBINATIONS BE SEEN MORE READILY? DOES THE CONSUMER LOOK DOWN FOR GRAPHIC INFORMATION (AS IN A GROCERY STORE) OR UPWARD (AS WHEN VIEWING MANY SIGNS)?

■ SHOULD INFORMATION BE DESIGNED DIFFERENTLY TO BE UNDERSTOOD FROM MOVING VEHICLES?

ACCOMMODATION ·

THE ULTIMATE DESIGN GOAL IS TO FIT, REACH, OR ACCOMMODATE ALL OF A TARGET AUDIENCE. YET IN REALITY, EFFECTIVE GRAPHICS REACH 90%+. NOTICE HOW DESIGN FOR ½ OF AN AUDIENCE EXCLUDES ½ OF IT. TRAFFIC SIGNS MUST REACH NEAR 100%.

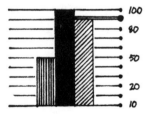

AUDIENCE %

TYPE SIZE ·

TYPE WITH A ONE INCH CAP HEIGHT CAN BE READ BY A STATIONARY AUDIENCE FROM FIFTY FEET. (HELVETICA, UNIVERSE) THE TYPE MUST BE HIGH CONTRAST MESSAGE/BACK-GROUND. THEREFORE 2" TYPE WOULD WORK AT 100 FEET. 6" TYPE IS FINE AT 300 FEET.

Ze — 1" HIGH

REVERSE TYPE ·

TYPE OR SYMBOLS WHICH ARE REVERSED (WHITE ON BLACK) LOOK ABOUT 10% LARGER THAN THOSE IN THE NORMAL (BLACK ON WHITE) RELATIONSHIP. THIS IS DUE TO THE PHENOMENON OF IRRADIATION. SIZE CHANGE THROUGH REVERSAL APPLIES TO HIGH CONTRAST COLOR PAIRS.

REVERSE

READING FLOW ·

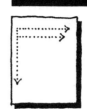

IN WESTERN CULTURES WE READ LEFT·TO·RIGHT/TOP·TO·BOTTOM. DESIGNERS NEED TO TAKE THIS EYE FLOW INTO ACCOUNT WHEN PLACING ELEMENTS ON A PAGE, PACKAGE, OR SCREEN.

EYE SCAN ·

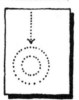

THE HUMAN EYE FAVORS THE LOWER LEFT HAND AREA OF ANY FIELD RATHER THAN THE CENTER OF THE FIELD AND WHEN SCANNING A FIELD TENDS TO FEEL COMFORTABLE IN THAT ZONE. THE EYE TENDS TO REST THERE AND RETURN THERE.

VISION ·

IN THE AUDIENCE FOR ANY VISUAL MESSAGE THERE ARE THOSE WITH FAULTY EYESIGHT. EYE GLASSES AND CONTACT LENSES CORRECT MOST PROBLEMS. YET NEARLY 6% OF THE MALE POPULATION HAS SOME DIFFICULTY WITH ACCURATE COLOR PERCEPTION. LESS THAN ½% OF THE POPULATION SEES NO COLOR WHATSOEVER.

HOW SMALL?

6 Point
7 Point
8 Point
9 Point
10 Point
11 Point

WHEN DESIGNING A BOOK OR PRODUCT-USE INSTRUCTIONS, BE CAREFUL OF TYPE SMALLER THAN 8 POINT. SMALLER MAKES READING UNCOMFORTABLE AND PERHAPS EVEN IMPOSSIBLE FOR OLDER PEOPLE. SMALL TYPE IS NOT EFFECTIVE UNDER LOW-LEVEL LIGHTING.

DESIGN FOR MOTION ·

WHEN DESIGNING MESSAGES TO BE READ FROM MOVING VEHICLES, TYPE MUST BE LARGER–3" HIGH AT 100 FEET AND AT LEAST 12" HIGH AT 400 FEET. MESSAGES MUST BE VERY SIMPLE–NO MORE THAN ONE PICTURE AND FEWER THAN SEVEN WORDS.

THE RIGHT TRACK

PROCESS

THE DESIGN PROCESS CAN BE AS SIMPLE AS MAKING A COLOR CHOICE OR AS COMPLEX AS FORMATTING A SERIES OF SCIENTIFIC TEXTBOOKS. IT CAN RANGE FROM SELECTING A TYPEFACE TO DESIGNING A GRAPHIC CONTROL DISPLAY FOR A MASSIVE WATER CONTROL PROJECT. ABOUT THE ONLY THING CONSTANT IN GRAPHIC PROBLEMS IS THE FACT THAT EACH PROBLEM HAS UNIQUE DIFFERENCES. YET CERTAIN COMMONALITIES DO HELP DESIGNERS TO STRUCTURE THEIR ATTACK ON A PROBLEM.

ALTERNATE SOLUTIONS · ANY PROBLEM HAS AN INFINITE NUMBER OF POSSIBLE VISUAL SOLUTIONS. IF WE CAN ACCEPT THIS FACT, AND CAN GENERATE VISUAL ALTERNATIVES, A GOOD DEAL OF OUR DESIGN ACTIVITY CAN INVOLVE MAKING VISUAL CHOICES.

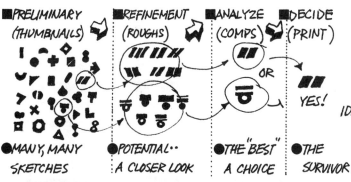

■ PRELIMINARY (THUMBNAILS) ■ REFINEMENT (ROUGHS) ■ ANALYZE (COMPS) ■ DECIDE (PRINT)

OR   YES!

● MANY, MANY SKETCHES   ● POTENTIAL·· A CLOSER LOOK   ● THE "BEST" A CHOICE   ● THE SURVIVOR

LINEAR PROCESS · ONE STAGE FOLLOWS ANOTHER IN A STRAIGHT LINE.

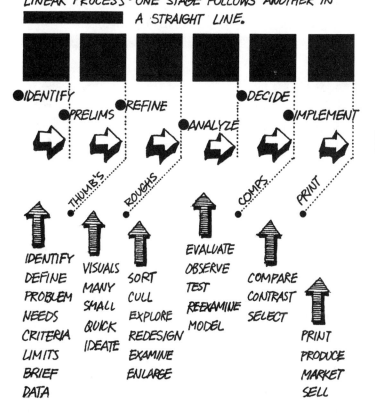

● IDENTIFY   ● PRELIMS   REFINE   ● ANALYZE   ● DECIDE   ● IMPLEMENT

THUMB'S   ROUGHS   COMPS.   PRINT

IDENTIFY
DEFINE
PROBLEM
NEEDS
CRITERIA
LIMITS
BRIEF
DATA

VISUALS
MANY
SMALL
QUICK
IDEATE

SORT
CULL
EXPLORE
REDESIGN
EXAMINE
ENLARGE

EVALUATE
OBSERVE
TEST
REEXAMINE
MODEL

COMPARE
CONTRAST
SELECT

PRINT
PRODUCE
MARKET
SELL

CYCLIC PROCESS · AFTER PROBLEM IDENTITY, PROCESS MOVES IN CIRCLE OR LIKE COIL SPRING.

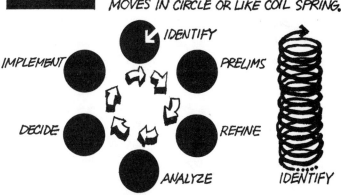

IDENTIFY
IMPLEMENT   PRELIMS
DECIDE   REFINE
ANALYZE   IDENTIFY

FEEDBACK PROCESS · LOOKING BACKWARD HELPS THE PROCESS ALONG. CONCURRENT PROGRESS. PROCESS GROWS BY CONSTANT CHECKING BACKWARDS THROUGH FEEDBACK LOOPS.

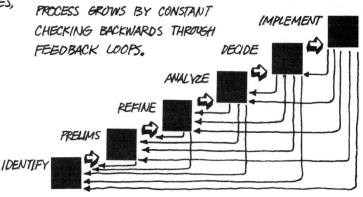

IMPLEMENT
DECIDE
ANALYZE
REFINE
PRELIMS
IDENTIFY

BRANCHING PROCESS · IDEA GROWS LIKE ROOT OR BRANCH. ANALYSIS AT EACH STAGE.

ANALYZE   ANALYZE   ANALYZE

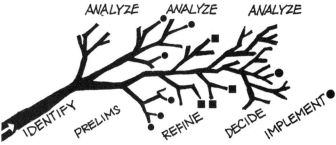

IDENTIFY   PRELIMS   REFINE   DECIDE   IMPLEMENT

PRIORITY PROCESS · IN THE DESIGN PROCESS, THE ESTABLISHMENT OF PRIORITIES IS ESSENTIAL. DESIGNERS MUST BE ABLE TO JUDGE AND GAUGE THE RELATIVE IMPORTANCE OF FACTORS AS THEY RELATE TO ONE ANOTHER. PRIORITIES SET THE FUNCTIONAL AND VISUAL CRITERIA IN COMMUNICATIONS.

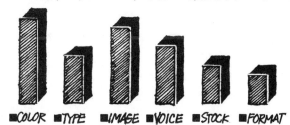

■ COLOR   ■ TYPE   ■ IMAGE   ■ VOICE   ■ STOCK   ■ FORMAT

GESTALT

Ge·stalt (gə-shtält′), *n.* [*pl.* GESTALTEN (-ən)], [G., lit., shape, form, configuration < MHG. *gestalt*, pp. of *stellen*, to arrange, fix, form], in *Gestalt psychology*, any of the integrated structures or patterns that make up all experience and have specific properties which can neither be derived from the elements of the whole nor considered simply as the sum of these elements.

Gestalt psychology, [see prec. entry], a school of psychology, developed in Germany, which affirms that all experience consists of Gestalten, and that the response of an organism to a situation is a complete and unanalyzable whole rather than a sum of the responses to specific elements in the situation.

GESTALT PERCEPTUAL FACTORS BUILD A VISUAL FRAME OF REFERENCE WHICH CAN PROVIDE THE DESIGNER WITH A RELIABLE PSYCHOLOGICAL BASIS FOR THE SPATIAL ORGANIZATION OF GRAPHIC INFORMATION. AROUND 1900, GERMAN AND AUSTRIAN PSYCHOLOGISTS BEGAN TO FORMULATE CONCEPTS BASED ON "PATTERN SEEKING" IN HUMAN BEHAVIOR. THEY DEVELOPED THEORY PARTICULARLY VALUABLE TO DESIGNERS AND PHOTOGRAPHERS. WE ARE DRAWN TO GESTALT PERCEPTUAL PSYCHOLOGY BECAUSE IT GIVES CONCRETE EVIDENCE OF HOW THE EYE ORGANIZES VISUAL EXPERIENCES.

THE GESTALT THEORY

1 THE <u>PARTS</u> OF A VISUAL IMAGE MAY BE CONSIDERED, ANALYZED, AND EVALUATED AS DISTINCT COMPONENTS.

2 THE <u>WHOLE</u> OF A VISUAL IMAGE IS DIFFERENT FROM AND <u>GREATER</u> THAN THE SUM OF ITS PARTS.

● EXAMPLES

■ WHEN YOU LOOK AT A PHOTOGRAPH OF A LANDSCAPE YOU MIGHT CONSIDER THE HILLS, SKY, SUNSET, LAKE, AND TREES AS ELEMENTS TO BE SEPARATELY ADMIRED. YET TAKEN TOGETHER THEY FORM A COHERENT WHOLE OF UNIFIED BEAUTY, EACH PART ADDING TO THE OTHER.

■ A POSTER MAY BE ANALYZED AS A RECIPE OF ILLUSTRATION, HEADLINE TYPE AND TEXT TYPE. WHEN THESE COMMUNICATION ELEMENTS ARE PLACED TOGETHER THEY REINFORCE ONE ANOTHER BUILDING A PATTERN THAT "GLUES" THE WHOLE.

■ THINK OF THIS MUSICAL ANALOGY: MUSICAL NOTES DEFINE A PATTERN OR MELODY. EACH NOTE MAY BE HEARD SEPARATELY AND CONSIDERED. IF THE NOTES ARE ARRANGED IN A PLEASING MELODY, THINK OF THE MELODY AS THE GESTALT WHICH IS GREATER THAN JUST THE SUM OF THE NOTES.

● A THOROUGH KNOWLEDGE OF VISUAL GESTALT PRINCIPLES GIVES THE GRAPHIC DESIGNER AN INVALUABLE TOOL BOX. WE KNOW THAT AUDIENCES WILL REACT TO OVERT OR OBVIOUS GESTALT PATTERNS. BY MATCHING A TARGET AUDIENCE WITH SELECTED HIGH IMPACT GESTALT IMAGES WE CAN SHORTEN THE DISTANCE TO EFFECTIVE COMMUNICATIONS. WE CAN, AS DESIGNERS, VIRTUALLY GUARANTEE AN AUDIENCE RESPONSE, WHICH IS THE BOTTOM LINE OF DESIGN EFFICIENCY. GESTALT IMAGERY CAN BE PHOTOGRAPHIC, SYMBOLIC, TYPOGRAPHIC, ILLUSTRATIVE OR A COMBINATION OF THESE. OVERT GESTALTS ARE PARTICULARLY USEFUL FOR GRAPHIC PIECES WHICH RELY ON QUICK EXPOSURE – POSTERS, MAGAZINE AND BOOK COVERS, AND TELEVISION GRAPHICS. TO WORK WITH GESTALT PRINCIPLES IN VISUAL IMAGERY IS TO DEAL WITH BASIC HUMAN RESPONSE, A NATURAL VISUAL ACTIVITY OF THE HUMAN ORGANISM.

■ GESTALT VISUAL PRINCIPLES HAVE LONG BEEN USED TO ANALYZE IMAGES. MOST FINE ARTS HAVE BEEN CONSIDERED FROM OTHER VIEWPOINTS : WITH RATHER MYSTICAL "ESTHETIC" JUDGEMENTS. GESTALT PRINCIPLES GIVE US THE OPPORTUNITY TO EVALUATE THE END EFFECTIVENESS OF VISUAL IMAGERY. DESIGNERS SHOULD THOROUGHLY LEARN GESTALT PERCEPTUAL PSYCHOLOGY AND EXPERIMENT WITH ITS EXCITING FORMS.

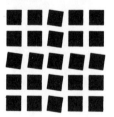

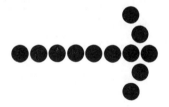

■ IN THIS ILLUSTRATION YOU CAN TEST YOUR NATURAL TENDENCY TO ORGANIZE VISUAL PATTERNS. SEE HOW YOU GROUP THE TILTED SQUARES AND SEE A CROSS OR PLUS.

■ HERE TWELVE DOTS HAVE BEEN ARRANGED TO FORM A DIRECTIONAL SYMBOL. WE CAN "SEE" EACH DOT SEPARATELY BUT THE ARROW IS GREATER THAN THE SUM OF THE DOTS AND BECOMES THE COLLECTIVE GESTALT.

1 FIGURE/GROUND · THE FUNDAMENTAL LAW OF PERCEPTION WHICH ALLOWS US TO "READ" IMAGERY. MADE POSSIBLE BY CONTRAST.
■ FIGURES · POSITIVE ELEMENTS DEFINED BY SPATIAL RELATIONSHIPS WHICH EXIST AMONG ALL THEIR PARTS. THEY OCCUR ON A FIELD OR GROUND.
■ GROUND · BACKGROUND, FIELD, WHITE SPACE, NEGATIVE SPACE, FORMAT WHICH CARRIES VISUAL IMAGE.
■ WE ARE ABLE TO READ A SPEEDOMETER, WATCH, OR SIGN.
■ POLAR BEARS HAVE A WHITE CAMOUFLAGE.

GROUND SHAPE

FIGURE

2 EQUILIBRIUM · EVERY PSYCHOLOGICAL FIELD TENDS TOWARD ORDER, BALANCE, AND MAXIMUM EFFICIENCY. NATURAL PHENOMENA ACT ON MATERIALS, ORGANISMS. THE RESULTING SHAPES OF GRAVITY, HEAT, AND PRESSURE ARE USUALLY "CLOSED," COMPACT.
■ WATER ON A WAXED SURFACE CLUSTERS.
■ BUBBLES IN A SOFT DRINK ARE ROUNDED.
■ A STRETCHED MEMBRANE CONTRACTS INTO A CIRCLE.
■ MOLTEN METAL FORMS INTO A BALL SHAPE.
■ FLOWERS OPEN AND CLOSE FROM A CENTRAL CORE.

3 ISOMORPHIC CORRESPONDENCE · DEALS WITH THE RELATIONSHIP BETWEEN STRUCTURAL CHARACTERISTICS OF VISUAL FORM AND SIMILAR CHARACTERISTICS OF HUMAN BEHAVIOR. EXPERIENCES OF PEOPLE, BOTH PHYSICAL AND PSYCHOLOGICAL, ARE RECALLED AND TRIGGERED BY SPECIFIC VISUAL IMAGES.
■ AN ILLUSTRATION OF A BLOODY KNIFE RECALLS A CUT.
■ A PHOTO OF A RATTLESNAKE TRIGGERS GREAT FEAR.
■ A TELEVISION AD FOR A HAMBURGER STIMULATES HUNGER.
■ AN ANTI·WAR POSTER INCITES A GROUP TO RIOT.
■ AN INCOMPLETE AD INVITES VIEWERS TO IMAGINE A DREAM HOME ON THEIR PROPERTY.

IMAGINE YOUR DREAM HOME IN THIS SPACE

4 CLOSURE · CLOSED SHAPES ARE MORE VISUALLY STABLE THAN UNCLOSED SHAPES. WE HAVE A NATURAL TENDENCY TO CLOSE GAPS AND COMPLETE AN UNFINISHED FORM.
■ WE IMAGINE HOW A PLIERS, WRENCH, OR TWEEZERS CLOSES.
■ WE VISUALLY CLOSE A GATE IN AN OPEN CORRAL.

5 PROXIMITY · PERCEPTUAL GROUPINGS ARE FAVORED ACCORDING TO THE NEARNESS OF PARTS. CLOSER PARTS FORM GROUPS BY VISUALLY UNITING.
■ FOUR BLACK SWANS SWIMMING TOGETHER DRAW ATTENTION FROM A LARGE FLOCK OF BIRDS.
■ YELLOW CABS CLUSTER NEAR A HOTEL ENTRANCE.
■ IN A GARDEN, CLUSTERS OF FLOWERS DRAW THE EYE MORE READILY THAN SINGLE FLOWERS.

IN THIS ARRANGEMENT THE EYE GOES FIRST TO THE GROUP

6 CONTINUATION · ORGANIZATION IN PERCEPTION LEADS THE EYE TO CONTINUE ALONG AND BEYOND A STRAIGHT LINE OR CURVE.
■ A DIRECTIONAL ARROW POINTS THE EYE IN THE INTENDED DIRECTION.
■ WE ARE ABLE TO READ THE CIRCULAR TYPESETTING ON AN OFFICIAL SEAL.

7 SIMILARITY · IDENTICAL VISUAL UNITS WILL BE SEEN TOGETHER IN GROUPS. SIMILAR OBJECTS ARE DEFINED BY SHAPE, SIZE, COLOR, AND DIRECTION.
■ IN A HERD OF CATTLE WE PERCEIVE BLACK ANGUS AND RED HEREFORDS AS SEPARATE GROUPS.
■ A CAR MOVING AGAINST TRAFFIC ON A ONE·WAY STREET BECOMES IMMEDIATELY APPARENT.

  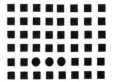

MARKS

GRAPHIC DESIGNERS HAVE A PROFESSIONAL
RESPONSIBILITY TO BE WELL VERSED IN THE
SPECTRUM OF MARKS AVAILABLE FOR SOLVING VISUAL
PROBLEMS. MANY CLASSIFICATION SYSTEMS EXIST,
DEVELOPED BY GRAPHIC DESIGNERS, ANTHROPOLOGISTS,
AND PSYCHOLOGISTS. MOST HAVE POSITIVE
ATTRIBUTES, BUT TAKEN TOGETHER THEY CAN LEAD
TO CONFUSION AND REDUNDANCY. A FEW BASIC
TERMS CAN EFFECTIVELY CLASSIFY MARKS AND FORM
A LOGICAL WORKING LANGUAGE FOR DESIGNER,
CLIENT, AND PRINTER.

1 SYMBOLS · MARKS WITHOUT TYPE USED TO
IDENTIFY A CORPORATION, AGENCY
OR INSTITUTION. CAN BE LEGALLY PROTECTED.

● ADVANTAGES:　　　　◆ DISADVANTAGES:
UNIQUE, SIMPLE GESTALT.　COSTLY TO PROMOTE, EXPLAIN.
QUICK IMPACT　　　　　CONFUSION WITH OTHER SYMBOLS

2 PICTOGRAPHS · PUBLIC SYMBOLS. USED TO CROSS
LANGUAGE BARRIERS FOR DIRECTION,
SAFETY, TRANSPORTATION. USE ENCOURAGED BY ALL.

● ADVANTAGES:　　　　◆ DISADVANTAGES:
SUBSTITUTE FOR WORDS.　CONFUSION WITH CORPORATE
INTERNATIONAL.　　　MARKS, CULTURAL CONFUSION.

3 LETTERMARKS · LETTERS FORM NAME IN TYPE.
USED TO IDENTIFY COMPANY,
OFTEN TO SHORTEN LONG NAME, NOT PRONOUNCEABLE.

● ADVANTAGES:　　　　◆ DISADVANTAGES:
LETTERFORMS READABLE.　COSTLY TO PROMOTE. HEAVY
ABBREVIATE NAME　　　VISUAL COMPETITION (LETTERS).

4 LOGOS · WORD OR WORDS IN TYPE. IDENTIFY
COMPANY, BRAND, PROJECT, GROUP.
PRONOUNCEABLE. CAN BE LEGALLY PROTECTED.

● ADVANTAGES:　　　　◆ DISADVANTAGES:
PHONIC, UNIQUE, EASIER　COMPLEX GESTALT, TYPE
TO PROMOTE　　　　　RELATION PROBLEMS.

5 COMBINATION MARKS · SYMBOL AND LOGO USED
TOGETHER. ALSO CALLED
SIGNATURE. CONSTANT SPACE RELATIONSHIP.

● ADVANTAGES:　　　　◆ DISADVANTAGES:
LABEL EFFECT. UNIQUE,　VERY COMPLEX GESTALT.
SMOOTH RECOGNITION.　REDUNDANT.

6 TRADEMARKS · ALL OF THE ABOVE. LEGAL
NAME FOR UNIQUE MARKS
WHICH MAY BE REGISTERED, PROTECTED BY LAW
AND SOLD IF DESIRED. FIRST COME, FIRST SERVED.

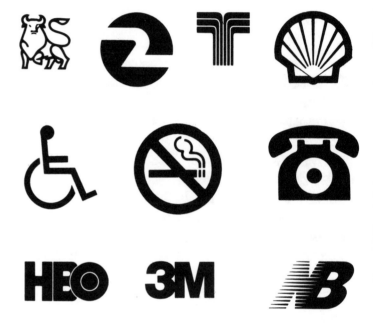

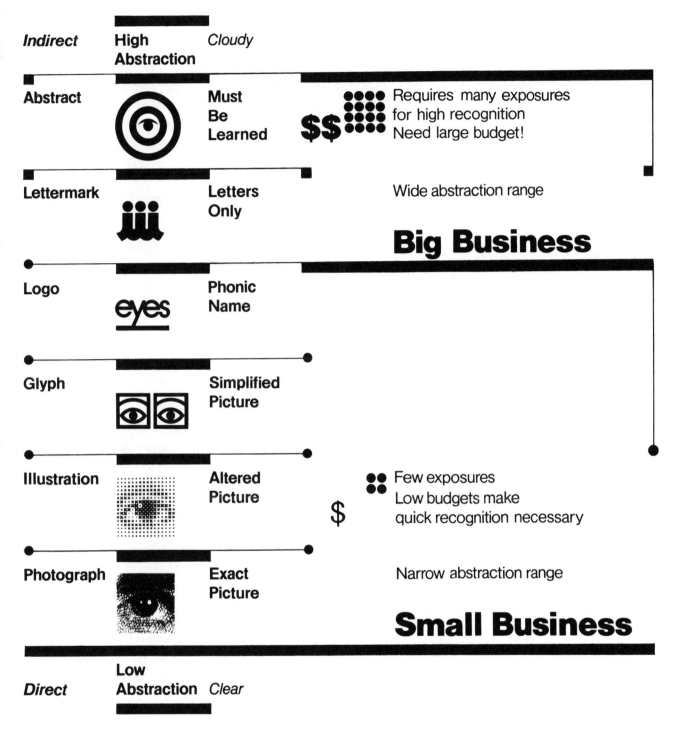

Indirect	High Abstraction	Cloudy		
Abstract		Must Be Learned	$$	Requires many exposures for high recognition Need large budget!
Lettermark		Letters Only		Wide abstraction range
				Big Business
Logo		Phonic Name		
Glyph		Simplified Picture		
Illustration		Altered Picture	$	Few exposures Low budgets make quick recognition necessary
Photograph		Exact Picture		Narrow abstraction range
				Small Business
Direct	Low Abstraction	Clear		

SELECTING AN EFFECTIVE MARK

TOO OFTEN DESIGNERS MAKE SERIOUS MISTAKES WHEN DEVELOPING AND PRESENTING MARKS TO CLIENTS, PARTICULARLY SMALL BUSINESSES. A GOOD CHECK POINT IS TO EVALUATE THE COMPANY BUDGET AND DETERMINE THE DOLLARS AVAILABLE FOR PROMOTION. IF A BUDGET IS VERY LARGE, THEN A HIGHLY ABSTRACT MARK IS A POSSIBILITY. MORE DOLLARS BUY MORE EXPOSURES OF THE MARK, WHICH TRANSLATES DIRECTLY INTO MARKET RECOGNITION. WHEN A BUDGET IS SMALL FEW EXPOSURES CAN BE PURCHASED, MAGNIFYING THE NEED FOR QUICK RECOGNITION AND LOW ABSTRACTION. A HIGH LEVEL OF ABSTRACTION IS A LUXURY ONLY THE HIGH-ROLLING CLIENT CAN AFFORD. LOW ABSTRACTION MARKS ARE QUICKER, MORE EFFECTIVE VISUAL TOOLS.

SYMBOLS

TRAITS OF "GOOD SYMBOLS" USEFUL FOR IDEATION, DEVELOPMENT, AND ANALYSIS.

1 POSITIVE ASSOCIATION · SYMBOL SHOULD SHOW THE IMAGE OF A COMPANY OR PRODUCT IN "BEST" OR FAVORABLE LIGHT.

2 EASY IDENTIFICATION · SYMBOL SHOULD QUICKLY AND READILY BE RECOGNIZED, REMEMBERED, AND RECALLED.

3 "CLOSE GESTALT" · THINK OF YOUR CLOSED HAND OR FIST AS "CLOSE GESTALT." WHEN YOU OPEN IT UP YOUR FINGERS POINT OUTWARD AND CREATE "OPEN GESTALT." EYE FLOW SHOULD BE INTERNAL RATHER THAN EXTERNAL.

"GOOD"   WEAK

THE PERFECT CIRCLE HAS IDEAL GESTALT AS IT SERVES AS A MAGNET FOR THE EYE.

4 ABSTRACTION LEVEL · SYMBOL MUST HIT THE APPROPRIATE UNDERSTANDING LEVEL OF THE INTENDED AUDIENCE. VERY ABSTRACT MARKS ARE COSTLY TO PROMOTE AND MAKE UNDERSTOOD. BEWARE! PHOTOGRAPHIC MARKS, ILLUSTRATED MARKS, AND LOGOS GENERALLY FUNCTION AS THE BEST COMMUNICATION ELEMENTS.

5 REDUCTION · SYMBOLS SHOULD BE DESIGNED TO REDUCE IN SIZE EFFECTIVELY TO $\frac{1}{2}$" IN DIAMETER. EVEN SMALLER WOULD BE BETTER. BE CAREFUL THAT THE SYMBOL DOES NOT LOSE PARTS AS IT BECOMES SMALLER. TEST REDUCTION SUCCESS ON VISUALIZER. USE STAT CAMERA FOR FINAL REDUCTION.

6 ONE COLOR · SYMBOLS SHOULD BE DESIGNED TO SUCCEED WITH ONE-COLOR PRINTING FOR ECONOMIC REASONS. COLOR MAY BE ADDED TO ENHANCE THE MARK BUT IT SHOULD NOT DEPEND ON COLOR FOR VISUAL SUCCESS. BE EXTREMELY CAREFUL OF SCREENS AND TINTS. THEY TEND TO EITHER FILL OR DISAPPEAR. THIS CAN BE CAUSED BY BOTH POOR CAMERA WORK AND LACK OF QUALITY CONTROL ON THE PRESS.
SYMBOLS WHICH RELY ON TWO OR MORE COLORS ARE VULNERABLE TO A WHOLE LIST OF "DEMONS."

7 NEGATIVE SPACES · A THOROUGH UNDERSTANDING OF THE FIGURE/GROUND PHENOMENON IS ESSENTIAL IN DESIGNING EFFECTIVE MARKS. NEGATIVE OR WHITE SPACES SHOULD BE CAREFULLY CONSIDERED. THESE WHITE SHAPES, THROUGH VISUAL POLARITY REVERSAL, CAN THEMSELVES BECOME MEMORABLE IMAGES (STAR, HEART, ETC.) WHICH HELP LEND THE SYMBOL ADDITIONAL MEANING.

8 SYMBOL WEIGHT · VISUAL WEIGHT OF THE SYMBOL SHOULD AS A RULE BE HEAVY. HEAVY MARKS TEND TO BE SIMPLER MARKS. HEAVY MARKS MORE SUCCESSFULLY WITHSTAND REDUCTION. HEAVY MARKS OFFER MORE CONTRAST TO SURROUNDING TYPE. LIGHT-WEIGHT MARKS MAKE WEAK STATEMENTS AND HAVE A MORE LIMITED RANGE OF EFFECTIVENESS.

9 FLOW · CONSIDER DESIGNING MARKS WHERE THE WHITE SPACE FLOWS RATHER THAN BECOMES TRAPPED. THE EYE THEN CAN MOVE THROUGH THE FORM RATHER THAN BE STOPPED BY IT.

SPACE TRAPPED HERE   EYE FLOWS THRU THIS MARK

10 DIRECTION · WHEN DIRECTIONAL INDICATION IS IMPORTANT IN A SYMBOL, POINTING UP AND TO THE RIGHT IS MORE EFFECTIVE THAN DOWN OR TO THE LEFT. THESE FORWARD, UPWARD DIRECTIONS ARE PERCEIVED AS POSITIVE BY THE VIEWING AUDIENCE.

NEGATIVE, DOWN, BACKWARDS, SLIPPING.   POSITIVE, UP, FORWARD, GAINING.

11 METERING · BUILD MARKS WITH A LIMITED VOCABULARY OF STRUCTURE. METER AND CONTROL LINES AND SPACES. BEWARE OF MIXING LINEAR AND SILHOUETTE FORMS!

METHODS

SYMBOLS CAN BE ANIMATE, INANIMATE, GEOMETRIC
ORGANIC, ILLUSTRATIVE, PHOTOGRAPHIC,
TYPOGRAPHIC, KINETIC.
THEY SHOULD INDICATE RATHER THAN DUPLICATE.
THEY SHOULD SUGGEST RATHER THAN REPRESENT.
SYMBOLS BECOME QUICK RECOGNITION DEVICES,
EFFECTIVE ONLY THROUGH REPETITION AND LEARNING.
VIRTUALLY ANY OBJECT, PRODUCT, COMPANY, CAUSE,
INSITUTION, RELIGION, OR FORCE CAN BE
SYMBOLIZED.

MANY PROCESSES AND TECHNIQUES ARE
USED TO CREATE SYMBOLS. A LOGICAL SEQUENCE
OF STAGES CAN SHORTEN THE PROCESS AND
INSURE SYMBOLS THAT WILL FUNCTION.
STAGES

PRELIMINARY SKETCHES · SMALL IDEA SKETCHES
ABOUT THE SIZE OF
YOUR THUMBNAIL ($\frac{1}{2}$" – $\frac{3}{4}$"). DRAWN
QUICKLY AND IN GREAT QUANTITY. THINKING
WITH YOUR PENCIL. FOR ONLY YOU AND YOUR
ART DIRECTOR, NOT THE CLIENT.

REFINED SKETCHES · LARGER SKETCHES.
REPRESENT THE BEST
FEW IDEAS. EDGES SHARPENED, DETAILS
CRISP, DRAWN WITH DRAFTING INSTRUMENTS.
TEST FEASIBILITY OF SYMBOL. DRAWN TO
SIZE APPROPRIATE TO THE INTRICACY
OF THE MARK.

PRESENTATION SKETCHES · FOR CLIENT VIEWING.
ABSOLUTELY PRECISE.
DRAWN WITH INSTRUMENTS, OFTEN REDUCTION
FROM LARGER ART·· PMT STAT. SOMETIMES
PRESENTED IN COLOR. A GOOD PRESENTATION SIZE
1" DIAMETER. CLIENT DECIDES WHETHER OR NOT
TO BUY THE SYMBOL HERE. ALSO CALLED "COMP"

1 RESEARCH · USE PHOTOGRAPHS, XEROX, MODELS.
COLLECT THE REAL AND DERIVE
FROM IT THE SYMBOLIC. USE RESEARCH TO
CONFIRM THAT YOUR IDEAS ARE ORIGINAL.

2 PAPER · USE LAYOUT PAPER, 25% RAG
BOND, TISSUE, AND/OR FROSTED
ACETATE. THE KEY IS TO HAVE A PAPER
SURFACE WHICH WILL HOLD A SHARP EDGE AND
GIVE SUFFICIENT TRANSLUCENCE FOR TRACING.

3 MEDIA · USE PENCIL (#2 OR #2.5) TO ROUGH
OUT SYMBOL IDEA. THEN REFINE
WITH A BLACK RAZOR TIP OR EXTRA FINE TIP
PEN. FIRST OUTLINE – THEN FILL. QUICK FILL
CAN BE DONE WITH A BOLD SHARPIE MARKER.

4 SIZE · PRELIMINARY SKETCHES SMALL.
$\frac{1}{2}$" DIAMETER WORKS WELL. BY
WORKING SMALL, FINE DETAIL IS AUTOMATICALLY
EDITED OUT. ALSO REPRODUCTION DIFFICULTIES
CAN BE PREDICTED. CONCEPTS CAN BE STUDIED
WITHOUT THE BURDEN OF FUSSY DETAIL. SMALL
SKETCHES ARE FAST. MORE IDEAS CAN BE
EXPLORED IN THE DESIGN STAGE.

5 TRACING · THIS IS A GREAT TIMESAVER WHEN
DEVELOPING A SYMBOL. USE A
LIGHT–TABLE OR WINDOW. TRACING IS MUCH
FASTER THAN DRAWING. IT IS ALSO A GREAT
TECHNIQUE FOR EXPLORING MANY IDEAS QUICKLY.
TRACING REALLY HELPS REFINEMENT AND EDITING.

6 ALTERNATIVES · SYMBOL SKETCHES ARE
ALTERNATIVE SOLUTIONS.
THEY REFLECT THE WAY A DESIGNER THINKS
WITH A PENCIL. THEY ALLOW YOU TO COMPARE
ONE IDEA TO ANOTHER. THE MORE YOU DO THE
BETTER YOUR CHANCES FOR DEVELOPMENT
AND AN EFFECTIVE SOLUTION.

7 ORGANIZATION · ORGANIZE YOUR SYMBOL
SKETCHES. USE A CONSISTENT
PAPER SHEET SIZE. ALLOW LOTS OF AIR AROUND
EACH SKETCH FOR EASY VIEWING. KEEP YOUR
SKETCHES SIMILARLY SIZED FOR UNBIASED
COMPARISON. SAVE YOUR SKETCHES. FILE THEM
CAREFULLY. THEY MAY BE USEFUL AS RESEARCH
ON FUTURE SYMBOL PROBLEMS.

SYMBOLS

CBS BY W. GOLDEN, N.Y. ABSTRACT EYE, PROMOTED VERY HEAVILY SINCE ABOUT 1951. EXTREMELY HIGH RECOGNITION BECAUSE OF EXPOSURE FREQUENCY. ONE OF BEST KNOWN MARKS IN U.S.

LITHOGRAPHIX BY DON WELLER AND DENNIS JUETT, LA. SHOWS MOVEMENT OF PRINTED IMPRESSION OFF PRESS. ALSO INCORPORATES HALFTONE SCREEN. DYNAMIC-MOVES THE EYE FORWARD, TO THE RIGHT.

ATLANTIC RICHFIELD COMPANY BY JOHN MASSEY, CHICAGO SUGGESTS AN ENERGY "SPARK" VERY ABSTRACT, DEMANDS CONSTANT EXPOSURE. ORIENTS ON A POINT SO LAYOUT OF MARK IS CRITICAL.

PAPA JOE'S BY DON WELLER, LA. THIS ILLUSTRATED SYMBOL IS A BEAUTIFUL FIGURE/GROUND STUDY. POTENTIALLY OMINOUS CHARACTER BECOMES FRIENDLY THROUGH USE OF HEART FORM. FOR A DINING/DRINKING EMPORIUM.

CANADIAN BROADCAST CORPORATION BY BURTON KRAMER, TORONTO. HIGH DEGREE OF ABSTRACTION. BOLD CAP C FRAGMENTS LIKE A SOUND WAVE. BOLD, DYNAMIC, AND PROMOTED HEAVILY. POSITIVE DIRECTION.

BICENTENNIAL '76 BY BRUCE BLACKBURN, N.Y. A UNIQUE RENDITION OF THE STAR/ STRIPES. GOOD FLOW WITHIN THE SYMBOL. ROUND EDGES SOFT, FRIENDLY.

PERFECTION AMERICAN BY GOLDSHOLL ASSOCIATES, NORTHFIELD, IL. MAKES STOCK GEARS FOR MACHINES. 3-D GEAR. STRONG OPTICAL CHARACTER. GOOD SPACE FLOW THRU THE SYMBOL.

METAMORPHOSIS BY GREGG BERRYMAN. WOMEN'S BOUTIQUE SYMBOL. RORSCHACH-LIKE THICK·THIN LINE SHAPES. REVERSE SHAPES SUGGEST FEMININITY, BODY DECORATION.

WOOLMARK BY FRANCESCO SAROGLIA, ITALY. SINCE 1964 HAS BECOME ONE OF THE WORLD'S MOST FAMILIAR SYMBOLS. ABSTRACTED SKEIN OF YARN, SPACE FLOW, OPTICAL STRENGTH. "WOOL·BLEND" MARK ITS'CHILD.

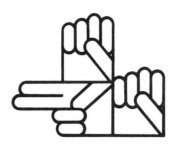

CSU/CHICO BY GREGG BERRYMAN
UNIVERSITY MARK. WIDELY EXPOSED.
INTENDED TO "SUGGEST" IMAGES
OF PLANT, TREE, BOOK, TORCH OF
LEARNING ·· SYMBOLS OF EDUCATION.
WHITE SHAPES FLOW OUT OF BOLD
CIRCLE.

SACRAMENTO HEARING SOCIETY
BY GAYLORD BENNITT. HANDS
SPELL OUT SIGN SIGNALS FOR
LETTERS SHS, SOCIETY INITIALS.
QUIET, LIGHT, LINE WEIGHT. NICE
CONNECTION BETWEEN TWO
COMMUNICATION SYSTEMS.

HEBREW RELIGIOUS ASSOCIATION
BY ROBERT PEASE, S.F. SIX-
POINTED STAR FORMS LEAF,
TREE. GOOD EYE FLOW THRU
SYMBOL SEGMENTS. UPWARD
LINE SLANTS SUGGEST
POSITIVE, HEAVENLY ASSOCIATION.

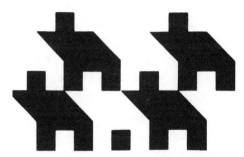

TIMBER MOUNTAIN DESIGN
BY DOUG POWELL, SACRAMENTO
BEAVER REPRESENTS FIRM
PRODUCING WOOD FURNITURE.
CONTINUOUS LINE SYMBOL
FEATURES ECONOMY OF FORM
AND A COMPACT GESTURE.

YOSEMITE NATIONAL PARK
BY G. DEAN SMITH, S.F.
DEPICTS HALF·DOME, PARK'S
MOST PROMINENT LANDMARK.
LINEAR SYMBOL WITH
CONTINUOUS WEIGHT. NATURAL
SHAPE REDUCED TO ESSENCE.

KLASSEN, CONTRACTOR BY
HARRY MURPHY, S.F. MODULAR
HOUSE SHAPES SUGGEST LARGE
DEVELOPMENT POTENTIAL.
FUNCTIONAL FIGURE/GROUND,
POLARITY SHIFT—BLACK TO
WHITE TO BLACK TO WHITE.

CHARACTER CULTIVATION LABS
BY R. KRUEGER, LA. MARK IS
DERIVED FROM A PHOTO WITH A
CIRCULAR LINE SCREEN. TOTAL
SENSORY IMPRESSION. DYNAMIC
EAR/SOUND/HEAD. MEMORABLE,
YET FACES BACKWARD.

CALIFORNIA CONSERVATION CORPS
BY MICHAEL VANDERBYL, S.F.
MOTHER AND CUB SUGGEST
"CARING" FOR THE ENVIRONMENT.
EFFICIENT WHITE SPACE
BECOMES CUB. DELICATE BALANCE,
YET STABLE BASE.

GRAND CANYON PARK BY
PRIMO ANGELI, S.F. SHOWS
TREMENDOUS DEPTH, FLAG
INDICATES NATIONAL TOURISM.
EYE OF VIEWER MUST WORK
TO SEE CANYON RIM. STRIPES
MEASURE DEPTH, CONTOURS.

LOGOS

log·o·type (lôg'ə-tīp', log'ə-tīp'), *n.* [*logo-* + *-type*], in *typography*, several letters, often making up a short word, cast in one piece but not united as in a ligature.

■LOGOS ARE MARKS WHICH CONSIST OF PRONOUNCEABLE WORDS. THEY ARE MOST OFTEN A SINGLE WORD SUCH AS "FORD", "COCA·COLA", OR "EXXON." THEY MAKE EXCELLENT IDENTITY DEVICES BECAUSE THEY ARE RELATED TO VISUAL AND PHONIC CODES WITH WHICH WE ARE FAMILIAR, UNLIKE ABSTRACT SYMBOLS. LOGOS MUST BE CAREFULLY RESEARCHED TO INSURE THAT THEY ARE CROSS·CULTURALLY EFFECTIVE, UNDERSTANDABLE, AND, MOST CRITICALLY, INOFFENSIVE. IDEALLY THEY ARE ONE WORD, THE SHORTER THE BETTER, TO PREVENT "OPEN GESTALT" PROBLEMS.

■TRAITS OF "GOOD LOGOS" ARE SIMILAR TO THOSE OF "GOOD SYMBOLS." IN ADDITION, THE DESIGNER MUST CONSIDER HOW THE LOGO SOUNDS AND HOW LETTERFORMS RELATE TO EACH OTHER (SINCE EACH LETTER IS IN ITSELF A SYMBOL). TO DESIGN EFFECTIVE LOGOS YOU SHOULD HAVE A THOROUGH GROUNDING IN TYPOGRAPHY. AS A RULE, LOGOS ARE MORE DIFFICULT TO DESIGN THAN SYMBOLS AND MORE TIME CONSUMING.

STAGES

TRACINGS · MOST SUCCESSFUL LOGOS ARE DERIVED FROM THE THOUSANDS OF EXISTING TYPEFACES. ON TISSUE OR BOND PAPER TRACE ALTERNATIVE LOGOS FROM TYPE SPECIMEN BOOKS. OUTLINE WITH A 2H PENCIL, FILL WITH A VERY SOFT BLACK PENCIL TO A TOTAL BLACKNESS. ALWAYS LIST TYPE NAME AND SPECIMEN PAGE NUMBER FOR FUTURE REFERENCE. THIS ALLOWS YOU TO SEE HOW YOUR LOGO WILL LOOK IN MANY TYPESTYLES. STAY SMALL AND FAST!

REFINEMENTS · OVERLAY TRACINGS FIRST IN SOFT PENCIL THEN IN BLACK MARKER. THIS ALLOWS YOU TO EXPLORE THE LIGATURES, DISTORTIONS, CASE VARIATIONS, AND SWASHES THAT MAKE THE LOGO TRULY UNIQUE.

PRESENTATION · PRESENT AS YOU WOULD A SYMBOL. ABSOLUTELY PRECISE. DRAW WITH DRAFTING INSTRUMENTS. TEST WITH VISUALIZER OR PMT STAT BEFORE FINAL COMPREHENSIVE STAT.

MOTHER CHILD

MOTHER AND CHILD BY HERB LUBALIN, N.Y. ORIGINALLY CREATED TO BE A MAGAZINE LOGO THE MARK DEPENDS ON LUBALIN'S HABIT OF ALTERING THE O IN LOGOS TO MAKE THEM UNIQUE. VERY WIDELY PUBLISHED, THIS LOGO FEATURES APPROPRIATE TYPE CHOICE, COMMON SERIFS, AND THE WOMB·LIKE SHAPE OF THE O FOR THE CHILD. CANNOT BE USED VERY SMALL BECAUSE OF THE TYPE WEIGHT OF "CHILD."

LA CASCADA BY RICHARDS GROUP, DALLAS. USES MODIFIED AVANT GARDE CAPS TO DESCRIBE A HIGH-QUALITY RESTAURANT CONTAINING WATER AND WATERFALLS. LOGICAL TREATMENT OF REPETITIVE LETTERFORMS. THE LOGO IS BUILT AROUND THE SIMPLIFIED CAP A. EXCELLENT CONTINUITY AND RHYTHM. SURPRISINGLY GOOD GESTALT FOR A NINE LETTER WORD, CAUSED IN PART BY THE FOUR A LIGATURES WHICH HELP REDUCE THE LOGO LENGTH.

ANZIO BY ALAN PECKOLICK, N.Y. DESIGNED FOR BOTH MOVIE AND BOOK. EXTRA BOLD SANS SERIF CAPS. BAYONET IMAGES REVERSE OUT OF TYPE. LETTERSPACING KEPT TIGHT TO FORM VIEWING GROUND. WEAPONS POINT FORWARD TO INDICATE A MARCH OR INVASION. LOGO HAS QUALITIES READILY ADAPTABLE TO ANIMATION FOR FILM. SUGGESTS THE VIOLENCE, REPULSIVE CHARACTER OF WAR. GIVES INSTANT IDENTITY TO THE STORY. AN EXTREMELY MEMORABLE LOGO WITH CLEAR DEMONSTRATION OF GESTALT.

OCEAN STATE BANK BY DON WELLER, L.A.
HAND DRAWN LETTERFORMS USE SWASHES
TO BUILD COHERENCE AND ADJUST
VISUAL WEIGHT. THEY GIVE A STRONG
SUGGESTION OF OCEAN WAVES, AND
ENCOURAGE VISUAL FLOW. STRONG,
COMPACT GESTALT. FRIENDLY.

DINERS QUEEN MARY BY ROGER
BARROWS, N.Y. HAND DRAWN SCRIPT
TYPE. SWASHES TURN INTO OCEAN
AND SERVE AS BASE FOR FAMOUS
SHIP WHICH SERVES AS LONG BEACH
TOURIST ATTRACTION. COMPLEX, BUT
GOOD GESTALT. REJECTED BY CLIENT.

ZOT'S BY GREGG BERRYMAN
CHAIN OF HOT DOG SHOPS.
"FRANKFURTER" TYPE FACE. STARS
SUGGEST AMERICAN ORIGIN OF
FOOD AND HIGH QUALITY OF
SANDWICHES. "BITE" HELPS
INDICATE "FAST FOOD."

HARP

HYALINE RESEARCH PROJECT BY
GERRY ROSENTSWIEG, L.A. USES OPEN
SAFETY PIN TO SIGNIFY INFANT
RESEARCH. THE PIN SPACES THE
H AND THE R AND ITSELF BECOMES
AN UPPER CASE A. GOOD CONTRAST
BETWEEN SERIF TYPE AND PIN.
UNIQUE, MEMORABLE, FOR A
RATHER DULL AND REMOTE
PROJECT TITLE.

Case

CASE IMPLEMENTS BY LIPPINCOTT &
MARGULIES, INC. N.Y. CREATED FOR A
PRODUCER OF HEAVY EQUIPMENT,
TRACTORS, LOADERS. STRONG
MASCULINE, INDUSTRIAL SHAPES.
LETTERS FORMED FROM NEGATIVE
SHAPES. EFFECTIVE FOR
STENCIL APPLICATIONS.

Art etc etc etc

ART, ETC. BY GREGG BERRYMAN
ART SUPPLIES AND MORE.
HELVETICA TYPE SLICED TO
RESEMBLE THE HIGHLIGHT ON
A FRAMED ART PIECE. MULTIPLE
ETCS. TO SUGGEST EXTREMELY
BROAD INVENTORY. PICTURE
FRAMING LARGE PART OF
BUSINESS.

DANSK BY ALAN PECKOLICK, N.Y.
FOR DANISH PRODUCER OF QUALITY
HOUSEWARES. GEOMETRIC LETTER-
FORMS REFLECT PRECISION,
ATTENTION TO DETAIL. COMPACT
GESTALT THRU TIGHT FITTING AND
OVERLAPPING.

EAT•N

EATON CORP. BY LIPPINCOTT & MARGULIES,
INC. N.Y. THIS LOGO FOR A CLEVELAND-
BASED CONGLOMERATE FORMERLY
KNOWN AS EATON YALE & TOWNE.
BOLD, CLEAN CAPS. LETTERFORMS
OVERLAP TO IMPROVE (CLOSE) GESTALT.
MOST UNIQUE QUALITY IS THE
"BONUS" A AND O, THAT WE SEE
ONLY IN THE FORMS OF THEIR
NEGATIVES OR COUNTERS. WIDELY
IMITATED BUT SELDOM WITH SUCCESS.

PBS

PUBLIC BROADCASTING SERVICE
BY ERNIE SMITH, N.Y.
TECHNICALLY A LETTERMARK
BUT HAS PHONIC QUALITY. HAND
DRAWN LETTERS USE SAME
SIZE CIRCLES AS COUNTER
SHAPES. HUMAN QUALITY BY
THE CONTOUR SHAPE OF THE
P. ONE OF THE BEST KNOWN
MARKS IN THIS COUNTRY.

PICTOGRAPHS

pic·to·graph (pik′tə-graf′, pik′tə-gräf′), *n.* [< L. *pictus* (see PICTURE); + -*graph*], 1. a picture representing an idea, as in primitive writing; hieroglyph. 2. writing of this kind.

■ PICTOGRAPHS ARE SYMBOLS WHICH REFER TO AN OBJECT, AN ACTION, A PROCESS, OR A CONCEPT. THEY ARE THE CHILDREN OF ANCIENT WRITING WHERE PICTURES TOOK THE PLACE OF WORDS. PICTOGRAPHS ARE VERY EFFECTIVE FOR BREAKING LANGUAGE BARRIERS. THEY ARE FREQUENTLY USED ON TRAFFIC SIGNS, AT INTERNATIONAL AIR TERMINALS, AT WORLD FAIRS, AT OLYMPIC GAMES AND IN MAJOR TOURIST CENTERS. WE SEE PICTOGRAPHS ON AUTOMOTIVE SWITCHES, FARM EQUIPMENT CONTROLS, AND ON OFFICE MACHINES, COPY MACHINES, AND COMPUTERS. THEY ARE USEFUL FOR SHIPPING INSTRUCTIONS, MAILING SYMBOLS, TECHNICAL MANUALS AND FOR CHART/GRAPH FUNCTIONS.

■ PICTOGRAPHS ENTERED THEIR MODERN PHASE IN 1909 WHEN SEVERAL EUROPEAN NATIONS DECIDED TO ADOPT PICTORIAL SYMBOLS FOR ROAD SIGNS.

■ PICTOGRAPHS ARE PUBLIC SYMBOLS AND ARE NOT OWNED BY A CORPORATION OR GOVERNMENT. USE OF PICTOGRAPHS IS ENCOURAGED, AND IN THE CASE OF TRAFFIC SIGNS IS MANDATORY BY LAW.

■ GOOD PICTOGRAPHS ARE VERY DIFFICULT TO DESIGN BECAUSE THEY MUST TRANSCEND TIME, STYLE, CULTURE, AND LANGUAGE. GRAPHIC DESIGNERS HAVE BEEN WORKING WITH PICTOGRAPHS FOR YEARS BUT THOSE DONE FOR THE 1964 TOKYO OLYMPICS BY KATZUMIE MARK THE FIRST SYSTEM WITH REAL GRAPHIC EXCELLENCE. BY FAR THE BEST U.S. SYSTEM TO DATE IS THE SYSTEM OF PICTOGRAPHS FOR THE DEPARTMENT OF TRANSPORTATION.

■ MORE WEAK PICTOGRAPHS EXIST THAN STRONG ONES. DESIGNERS NEED TO CAREFULLY SELECT A PICTOGRAPH WITH A TRACK RECORD, AS THE PUBLIC IS EASILY CONFUSED.

■ MOST PICTOGRAPHS DO NOT STAND ALONE. THEY ARE PART OF A SERIES OF SIGNS AND AS SUCH NEED TO BE VISUALLY WEIGHTED TO "LOOK" ALIKE.

■ PICTOGRAPHS HAVE THE SAME CRITERIA FOR EFFECTIVE FORM AS SYMBOLS. YET BECAUSE THEY OFTEN INVOLVE MORE THAN A SINGLE OBJECT, THEY ARE VISUALLY VERY COMPLEX. TEAMS GENERALLY DESIGN MORE EFFECTIVE PICTOGRAPHS THAN INDIVIDUAL DESIGNERS. GRAPHIC DESIGNERS HOWEVER SHOULD BE SKILLED IN SELECTING AND APPLYING PICTOGRAPHS.

● EUROPEAN TRAFFIC PICTOGRAPHS. COMMON THROUGHOUT THE CONTINENT. MANY VARIATIONS EXIST. SOME PRESENT VISUAL PROBLEMS. ONE FLAW IS THE RAIL SIGN SHOWN HERE. TECHNOLOGY HAS MADE THE STEAM LOCOMOTIVE OBSOLETE, SO THE ANTIQUE FORM LOSES ITS CURRENT VISUAL ASSOCIATION.

● COMMON U.S. TRAFFIC SIGNS WHICH ARE PICTOGRAPHS. THESE SIGNS WERE DESIGNED BY TRAFFIC ENGINEERS, NOT GRAPHIC DESIGNERS AND THAT IS REFLECTED IN FORMS AND WEIGHT. VERY ORDINARY!

● PICTOGRAPHS FOR SPORTS EVENTS BY THE JAPANESE DESIGNER KATZUMIE. INTRODUCED DURING THE 1964 TOKYO OLYMPICS. A STANDARD. BY A TEAM OF 30 DESIGNERS.

● THE PICTOGRAPHS BELOW BY LANCE WYMAN FOR THE 1968 OLYMPICS IN MEXICO CITY INDICATE WELL KNOWN LANDMARKS IN THE URBAN AREA.

●THIS SYSTEM OF WINTER SPORTS MARKS WERE DESIGNED FOR THE WINTER OLYMPICS IN GRENOBLE, FRANCE IN 1968 BY ROGER EXCOFFON, FRANCE. UNIQUE BECAUSE OF THEIR LIVELY, KINETIC LOOK WHICH CAPTURES THE MOVEMENT OF THE EVENT. THESE PICTOGRAPHS HAVE A 50/50 FIGURE/ GROUND RATIO, MAKING THEM ACTIVE.

●THE WELL KNOWN DEPARTMENT OF TRANSPORTATION PICTOGRAPHS. DESIGNED BY THE AIGA GROUP (GEISMAR, MEYER, COOK, ETC.). THIS SYSTEM OF TWENTY MARKS REPRESENTS THE "CREAM" OF ALL SIMILAR SYSTEMS. ANALYZED, TESTED, AND REDRAWN FOR VISUAL WEIGHT, BALANCE. THESE HAVE BEEN ADOPTED AT MOST MAJOR U.S. AIR TERMINALS AND WILL BE MORE WIDESPREAD IN YEARS TO COME. A GOOD SYSTEM TO MEASURE OTHER PICTOGRAPHS BY.

●U.S. NATIONAL PARKS SERVICE SYSTEM. DESIGNED BY CHERMAYEFF/GEISMAR OF NEW YORK. THEY ARE IN WIDE USE AT YOSEMITE, LASSEN, YELLOWSTONE ETC.

19

IDENTITY

VISUAL IDENTITY IS THE VISIBLE ESSENCE OF A CORPORATION, INSTITUTION, OR GOVERNMENT AGENCY. IDENTITY, UNIFIED AND CONTROLLED, CAN PROVIDE A POSITIVE ASSOCIATION WITH AN ORGANIZATION IN THE EYES OF EMPLOYEES, CUSTOMERS, STOCKHOLDERS, AND THE PUBLIC.

■ INTEGRATED VISUAL IDENTITY CAN WORK WELL FOR A SMALL SHOP, OR LARGE CORPORATION WITH HUNDREDS OF THOUSANDS OF EMPLOYEES AND A MULTI-BILLON DOLLAR ANNUAL BUDGET.

■ THE CONCEPT OF VISUAL COHERENCE DATES BACK TO EARLY GUILDS (WEAVERS, METALSMITHS, ETC.) PROFESSIONAL DESIGNERS HAVE WORKED WITH IDENTITY IN THIS COUNTRY SINCE THE 1920'S, BUT WITH DISTINCTION ONLY SINCE THE END OF WW2.

■ THE LANDMARK CORPORATE DESIGN PROGRAMS WERE FOR THE MOST PART DONE IN THE 50'S AND 60'S (IBM, EASTERN AIR LINES, XEROX, MOBIL, RCA, BELL SYSTEM, WESTINGHOUSE, ETC.). THE '70'S HAVE SEEN THE IDENTITY CONCEPT FILTER DOWN TO SMALLER CORPORATIONS AND BECOME ALMOST UNIVERSALLY ACCEPTED. THIS HAS ALSO BEEN THE DECADE OF GOVERNMENT ACCEPTANCE (NASA, DEPT. OF LABOR, INTERNAL REVENUE).

1 RESEARCH

THE FIRST STEP IN THE IDENTITY PROCESS INVOLVES A CAREFUL ANALYSIS OF EXISTING VISUAL IDENTITY OF AN ORGANIZATION. SAMPLES AND PHOTOGRAPHS ARE COLLECTED, EXAMINED, RATED. INTERVIEWS ARE CONDUCTED INTERNALLY AND EXTERNALLY. COMPETITION IS STUDIED AND EVALUATED. TARGET MARKETS ARE DEFINED. ALL TOOLS ARE BROUGHT TO BEAR ON KNOWING AS MUCH AS POSSIBLE ABOUT THE ORGANIZATION.

■ FINALLY A BRIEF, REPORT, OR PROPOSAL IS GENERATED OUTLINING THE VISUAL IDENTITY'S JUSTIFICATION, SCOPE, BUDGET AND DESIGN PROCEDURE. ON VERY LARGE PROJECTS, OUTSIDE MARKET RESEARCH FIRMS ARE EMPLOYED TO HANDLE THE TASK. RESEARCH MAY VARY FROM A COUPLE OF HOURS TO A YEAR OR MORE.

■ RESEARCH, SOLIDLY DONE, OFTEN GREATLY SIMPLIFIES THE REMAINDER OF THE PROCESS. IN THESE DAYS OF MULTI-NATIONAL ORGANIZATIONS, CROSS-CULTURAL VISUAL RESEARCH IS ESSENTIAL.

2 CORE IDENTITY

■ RESEARCH IS CONVERTED INTO VISUAL MATERIAL. CORE IDENTITY INCLUDES MARK (SYMBOL OR LOGO), COLOR, TYPE SYSTEM, SIGNATURES, AND PERHAPS LEGAL SEAL. CORE IDENTITY REFLECTS THE SUM TOTAL OF ALL SKETCHES REFINED TO ALTERNATIVE COMPS FOR PRESENTATION TO THE CLIENT. THE FINAL INTENT IS TO "SELL" BEST ALTERNATIVE. CORE IDENTITY IS THE FOUNDATION FOR ANY VISUAL IDENTITY PROGRAM.

3 APPLICATION

■ APPLICATION OF THE CORE IDENTITY INVOLVES EXTENDING A UNIFIED VISUAL IMAGE OR UMBRELLA OVER THE ENTIRE SPECTRUM OF AN ORGANIZATION'S BUSINESS SYSTEM, PROMOTIONS, PACKAGES, SIGNAGE, VEHICLES, ANNUAL REPORTS, ADVERTISING, UNIFORMS, AND ARCHITECTURE. EACH APPLICATION IS A DESIGN PROBLEM IN ITS OWN RIGHT, BUT SOLID CORE IMAGERY PROVIDES A STARTING POINT FOR EACH TASK.

4 CONTROL

■ IDENTITY CONTROL INVOLVES OVERSEEING AND MANAGING ALL VISUAL APPLICATIONS. THIS IS OFTEN DONE IN A LARGE ORGANIZATION BY A HIGH-LEVEL MANAGER AND A PRECISE CONTROL MANUAL TO EXPLAIN APPLICATION SITUATIONS. CONTROL DETERMINES THE ULTIMATE SUCCESS OF ANY VISUAL IDENTITY PROGRAM, LARGE OR SMALL.

SYSTEMS

■ BUSINESS SYSTEMS ARE IN MOST SITUATIONS THE FIRST ELEMENTS COMPLETED IN THE VISUAL IDENTITY PROCESS. THEY MAKE IDEAL PRESENTATIONS FOR CONVEYING CORE IDENTITY CONCEPTS TO THE CLIENT. BUSINESS SYSTEMS ARE UNIVERSAL, AND PROPER DESIGN CAN MAKE THEM INVALUABLE IDENTITY VEHICLES.

SIZE

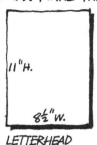 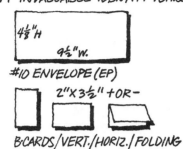

11"H.
8½"W.
LETTERHEAD

4⅛"H
9½"W.
#10 ENVELOPE (EP)

2"X3½" +OR-
B·CARDS/VERT./HORIZ./FOLDING

■ THESE "STANDARD" SIZE UNITS ARE BY FAR THE MOST COMMON ALTHOUGH OTHERS ARE USED. A COMMON SMALLER SIZE IS THE "MONARCH", USED FOR PERSONAL, MEMO, AND EXECUTIVE SYSTEMS (LETTERHEAD 7¼X10½, EP. 3⅞ X 7½)

GRAPHIC ZONES

THESE SKETCHES INDICATE POSSIBLE ZONES FOR PLACING GRAPHIC ELEMENTS ON THE SYSTEM.

■ HATCHED AREAS INDICATE POTENTIAL LAYOUT AREAS. WHITE AREA ON THE LETTERHEAD SHOWS TYPEWRITER TERRITORY, ON ENVELOPE INDICATES FEDERAL POSTAGE AREA AND GRIPPER EDGES. NO SPACE OFF·LIMITS ON THE BUSINESS CARD DUE TO PRESS SHEET SIZE.

THE SYSTEMS DESIGN APPROACH · START WITH THE SMALLEST ELEMENT IN THE PACKAGE, THE BUSINESS CARD. DESIGN ELEMENTS (SYMBOL, TYPE SIZE/COMPOSITION SYSTEM, SIGNATURE SPACES, COLOR, PAPER, MARGINS, ETC.) SHOULD BE CONSISTENT FROM PIECE TO PIECE. THE SYSTEM SHOULD FUNCTION IN THE TYPEWRITER AND CONVEY A UNIFIED ASSOCIATION WITH THE ORGANIZATION.

THESE SKETCHES SHOW SIMILAR MARGINS, ELEMENT SIZE, POSITION. THE TYPING MARGIN IS DEFINED ON LETTERHEAD.

SYSTEM INFORMATION

TYPOGRAPHIC INFORMATION ON BUSINESS SYSTEMS VARIES BUT CERTAIN COPY IS A REQUIREMENT.

■ LETTERHEAD

COMPANY NAME● → DESIGN PLUS
STREET ADDRESS● → 12 OAK PLAZA
CITY/STATE/ZIP● → BEND, OREGON, 47388
TELEPHONE● → (503) 218-6624

FOR MOST ENVELOPES, THE TELEPHONE NUMBER IS OMITTED. FOR MOST BUSINESS CARDS TWO ADDITIONAL LINES OR ITEMS ARE ADDED.

NAME● → JAY HOOK
TITLE● → ART DIRECTOR

■ THESE 4, 3, AND 6 LINE ITEMS ARE THE SKELETAL INFORMATION FOR MOST SYSTEMS. OCCASIONALLY, PRODUCTS, SERVICES, SECONDARY ADDRESSES, ETC. ARE ADDED. BE CAREFUL NOT TO CROWD THE SYSTEM WITH INFORMATION BEST LEFT TO OTHER PROMOTIONS.

DESIGN FOR TYPING · ALWAYS DESIGN SO THE SYSTEM WILL FIT THE TYPEWRITER. POSITION OF DESIGN ELEMENTS WILL DETERMINE HOW THE FINISHED PIECES WILL LOOK. KEEP FOLDS IN MIND.

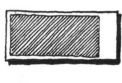

■ BLOCK STYLE LETTER
● DATE ● FOLD
● INSIDE ADDRESS
● BODY
● SIGNATURE
● MARGINS VARY FROM ¾" TO 3" BUT 1½" IS MOST COMMON

SYSTEMS FORMATS

· AN INFINITE NUMBER OF LAYOUT POSSIBILITIES EXIST. EXPLORE!

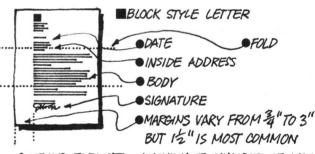

TYPE

ty·pog·ra·phy (tī-pog′rə-fi), *n.* [Fr. *typographie;* ML. *typographia;* see TYPO- & -GRAPHY], 1. the art of printing with type. 2. the setting and arranging of types and printing from them. 3. the arrangement, style, or general appearance of matter printed from type. Abbreviated **typ., typo., typog.**

■ THE APPLICATION OF DESIGN PRINCIPLES TO THE SETTING OF TYPE.

■ CHOOSING AND USING TYPE.

■ DESIGNING WITH TYPE... NOT THE DESIGNING OF TYPE.

■ "GOOD TYPOGRAPHY IS A FUSION OF INFORMATION AND INSPIRATION, OF THE CONSCIOUS AND UNCONSCIOUS, OF YESTERDAY AND TODAY, OF FACT AND FANTASY, WORK AND PLAY, CRAFT AND ART." ● PAUL RAND

CLASSIFICATION · OVER TEN THOUSAND TYPE FACES EXIST. SEVERAL THOUSAND ARE AVAILABLE AT A GIVEN TIME. SEVERAL CLASSIFICATION SYSTEMS EXIST. THIS ONE IS LOGICAL.

SERIF · HORIZONTAL STROKES AID READING. THICK· THIN CONTRAST.

ABCDEFGH
abcdefghijkln

typ
SERIF
SERIF

SANS · SERIF · SIMPLE, UNIFORM STROKE WIDTH, CLEAN.

ABCDEFGH
abcdefghijk

Aa
NO SERIFS

SCRIPT · DESIGNED TO SIMULATE HANDWRITING. VERY LITTLE CONTRAST BETWEEN THICK THIN STROKES. LETTERS CONNECT, FLOW, ARE USUALLY INCLINED.

ABCDEF
abcdefghijk

TEXT LETTERS · RESEMBLE HAND DRAWN LETTERS OF SCRIBES. LETTER FORMS SIMILAR TO THOSE OF CALLIGRAPHY.

𝕬𝕭𝕮𝕯𝕰𝕱𝕲
abcdefghijkl

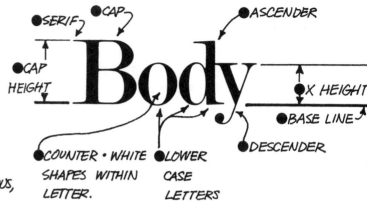

● SERIF   ● CAP   ● ASCENDER

● CAP HEIGHT

Body

● X HEIGHT

● BASE LINE

● DESCENDER

● COUNTER · WHITE SHAPES WITHIN LETTER.

● LOWER CASE LETTERS

TYPE MEASUREMENT

■ VERTICAL · POINT ($\frac{1}{72}$") THE LARGER THE POINT NUMBER, THE TALLER THE TYPE.

TEXT SIZES

6	ABCDEFGHIJKLMNOPQRSTUVWXYZABCDEFGH
8	ABCDEFGHIJKLMNOPQRSTUVWXYZA
10	ABCDEFGHIJKLMNOPQRSTUV
12	ABCDEFGHIJKLMNOPQR

HEAD SIZES

14	ABCDEFGHIJKLMNO
18	ABCDEFGHIJKLM
24	ABCDEFGHI
30	ABCDEFG
42	ABCDE

■ HORIZONTAL · PICA ($\frac{1}{6}$") THE MORE PICAS THE LONGER THE LINE OF TYPE.

Printers' Measurements

The *point* and the *pica* are two units of measure universally used in printing in all English-speaking countries. Today, not only is the *point system* used to measure type sizes, it is also used to mark up copy for typesetting: measure (length of line), line spacing, dimensions of type area, etc.

20 PICA LINE ($3\frac{5}{16}$")

■ EM · SQUARE OF THE TYPE SIZE. A 48 POINT EM IS A 48 POINT SQUARE. ONE EM IS COMMON MEASURE FOR INDENTING A PARAGRAPH.

UNIT · MEASURE USED FOR PHOTO- TYPESETTING. COMES FROM DIVIDING EM INTO VERTICAL UNITS. MORE DIVISIONS ALLOW GREATER PRECISION IN LETTERSPACING, WORD SPACING. HERE A 64 POINT EM IS DIVIDED INTO 18 UNITS.

22

LETTERSPACING · INVOLVES THE AMOUNT OF SPACE ▊▊▊ BETWEEN INDIVIDUAL LETTERS AND PUNCTUATION CHARACTERS. EXCELLENT, CONSISTENT LETTERSPACING IS THE KEY TO THE PROFESSIONAL HANDLING OF TYPE. A THOROUGH UNDERSTANDING OF FIGURE/GROUND IS ESSENTIAL. TYPE SHAPES HAVE DISTINCT QUALITIES. THEY FIT TOGETHER IN MANY, MANY COMBINATIONS. (THINK OF HOW MANY WORDS ARE IN THE DICTIONARY!)

FOUR KINDS OF STROKES MAKE UP LETTERFORMS. THESE MUST BE SPACED IN A LOGICAL, CONSISTENT MANNER TO APPEAR OPTICALLY CORRECT. THE IDEA IS TO MAINTAIN COMFORTABLE OPTICAL VOLUMES (FIGURE/GROUND) BETWEEN LETTERFORMS. EACH LETTER SHOULD "FLIRT" WITH THE ONE NEXT TO IT.

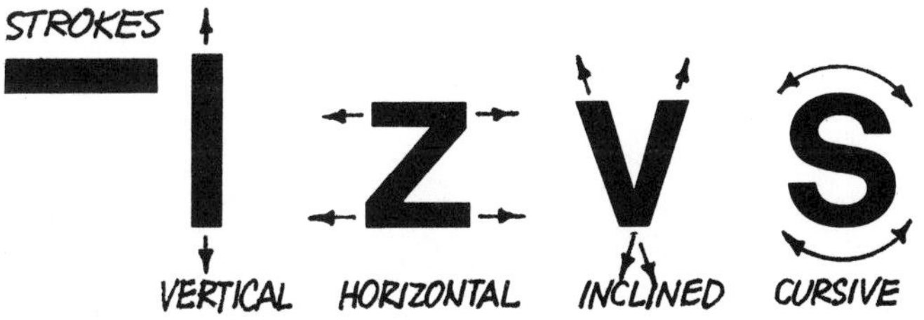

STROKES

l z v s

VERTICAL   HORIZONTAL   INCLINED   CURSIVE

OPTICAL VOLUMES · TRY TO MAKE THESE VOLUMES ▊▊▊ "LOOK" EQUAL.
THINK OF POURING ROUGHLY EQUAL VOLUMES OF SAND OR SALT BETWEEN LETTERS.

hiktoey

LETTERSPACING SCALE · TO LETTERSPACE WELL YOU ▊▊▊ NEED VISUAL BENCHMARKS. SHOWN HERE ARE THE EXTREME SPACING LIMITS. BUILD YOUR OWN LETTERSPACING SYSTEM AND ACHIEVE CONSISTENCY.

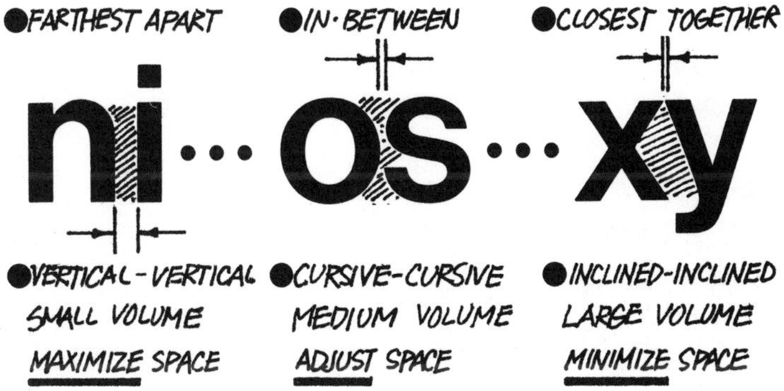

● FARTHEST APART   ● IN·BETWEEN   ● CLOSEST TOGETHER

ni···os···xy

● VERTICAL-VERTICAL   ● CURSIVE-CURSIVE   ● INCLINED-INCLINED
SMALL VOLUME   MEDIUM VOLUME   LARGE VOLUME
MAXIMIZE SPACE   ADJUST SPACE   MINIMIZE SPACE

BASE · CURSIVE LETTERS ARE DESIGNED SLIGHTLY ▊▊▊ TALLER THAN STRAIGHT STROKE LETTERS SO THEY WILL "LOOK" EXACTLY THE SAME HEIGHT. CURSIVE LETTERS MUST BE PLACED SLIGHTLY BELOW THE BASELINE SO THEY WILL APPEAR TO BE ON THE LINE.

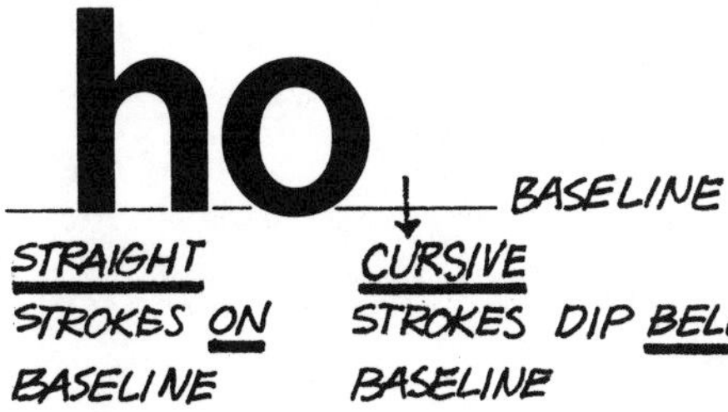

ho ──↓── BASELINE

STRAIGHT   CURSIVE
STROKES ON   STROKES DIP BELOW
BASELINE   BASELINE

HANGING · CURVED LETTERS, INCLINED LETTERS, ▊▊▊ AND SOME HORIZONTAL LETTER STROKES SITUATE BEYOND THE VERTICAL OR LEFT·HAND MARGIN. THIS IS SO THAT THEY WILL APPEAR TO BE ON THE MARGIN. PUNCTUATION CAN ALSO HANG. DESIGNERS MUST BE CONCERNED WITH HANGING WHEN ADJUSTING HEADLINE TYPE.

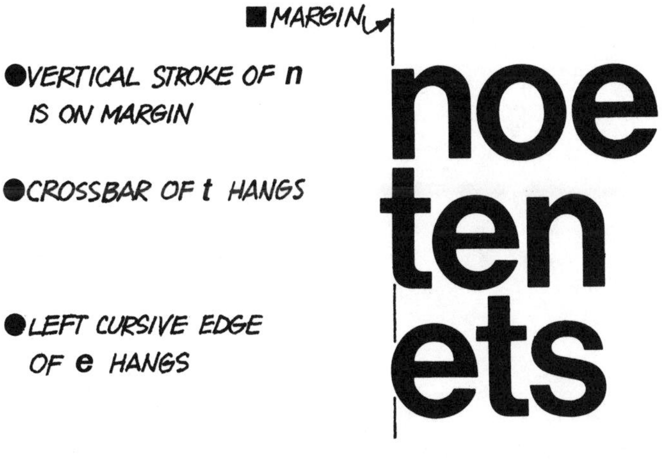

■ MARGIN ↵

● VERTICAL STROKE OF n IS ON MARGIN

● CROSSBAR OF t HANGS

● LEFT CURSIVE EDGE OF e HANGS

**noe
ten
ets**

KERNING · INVOLVES SELECTIVELY REDUCING ▊▊▊ THE SPACE BETWEEN CHARACTERS WHILE LEAVING THE REST OF THE SETTING THE SAME. BECAUSE OF THEIR LETTER SHAPES, CERTAIN COMBINATIONS SUCH AS Yo, Te, AW REQUIRE EXTREME SPACE ADJUSTMENTS. KERNING AFFORDS ADDITIONAL TYPOGRAPHIC SOPHISTICATION.

NORMAL
LETTERSPACE   **To   Ye   Av**

KERNED   **To   Ye   Av**

NOTICE HOW THE KERNED LETTERS SNUGGLE TO REDUCE EXCESSIVE SPACE VOLUMES.

TYPE

WORDSPACING · WORDS BEGIN AND END WITH DIFFERENT SHAPE LETTERS. WORDSPACING SHOULD MAKE ALL THE SPACE INTERVALS BETWEEN WORDS "LOOK" THE SAME. VOLUMES ARE ADJUSTED AS IN LETTERSPACING BY OPTICAL EXAMINATION. THE SPACES, HOWEVER, ARE LARGER AND AT FIRST ARE MORE DIFFICULT TO ADJUST. SPACE MUST VARY WITH THE SHAPE OF BEGINNING AND ENDING LETTERS AND WITH THE TYPEFACE USED. WORDS MUST NOT APPEAR TO RUN TOGETHER OR BE SPACED SO WIDELY AS TO APPEAR TO BE SEPARATE UNITS.

■ ONE SYSTEM IS TO IMAGINE A LOWER CASE n BETWEEN WORDS <u>WITHOUT</u> LETTERSPACING. THIS GIVES A MODERATE WORDSPACING.

quick brown fox

■ ANOTHER SYSTEM IS TO IMAGINE THE LOWER CASE i <u>WITH</u> LETTERSPACE TO EACH SIDE. THIS GIVES A TIGHTER WORDSPACING.

set up

It's time we all went on an energy diet.

Majority of smokers matches taste of leading

So Sandra knows her job. And She says she's never had one unpleasant those hundreds of trips. Cross her

■ TOO MUCH OR TOO LITTLE WORDSPACING MAKES READING DIFFICULT. WORDSPACING SHOULD VARY WITH TYPEFACE, TYPE SIZE, AND TYPE ARRANGEMENT. WORDSPACING AND LETTERSPACING SHOULD BE CONSISTENT. TIGHT LETTERSPACING DEMANDS TIGHT WORDSPACING. SPECIFY WITH <u>LOOSE</u>, <u>NORMAL</u>, <u>TIGHT</u>, <u>VERYTIGHT</u>.

LINESPACING · OFTEN CALLED <u>LEADING</u>, THIS IS THE VERTICAL SPACE BETWEEN LINES OF TYPE. LINESPACING IS MEASURED IN POINTS. THE CLOSEST LINESPACING IS CALLED MINUS LEADING, AND INVOLVES THE REDUCTION OF SPACE BETWEEN LINES. SETTING SOLID IS WHEN LINESPACING HAS BEEN NEITHER ADDED NOR SUBTRACTED. BEWARE OF EXCESSIVE LEADING WITH HEADLINE TYPE. LINESPACING MUST TAKE INTO ACCOUNT CHARACTER ASCENDERS AND DESCENDERS AND INSURE THAT THEY DO NOT OVERLAP.

The amount of space between
There is no set rule to follow.
sometimes be as bad as not
→ SET SOLID

The amount of space between
There is no set rule to follow.
sometimes be as bad as not
→ 1 POINT LINESPACING

The amount of space between
There is no set rule to follow.
sometimes be as bad as not
→ 2 POINT LINESPACING

The amount of space between
There is no set rule to follow.
sometimes be as bad as not
→ 3 POINT LINESPACING

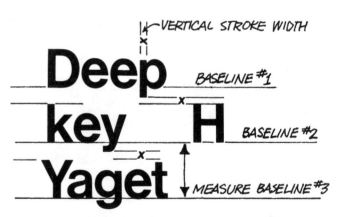

Deep key Yaget

HERE IS A SYSTEM FOR COMFORTABLE HEADLINE LEADING WHICH INSURES ASCENDERS AND DESCENDERS WON'T CLASH OR OVERLAP.
● ESTABLISH BASELINE #1.
● MEASURE VERTICAL STROKE WIDTH FROM BOTTOM OF DESCENDER.
● POSITION CAPITAL H AS SHOWN. BOTTOM OF H DETERMINES BASELINE #2.
● MEASURE BASELINE #3 AND ALL OTHERS.

THE TRUE TEST OF AN EXCELLENT TYPEFACE IS THAT IT CAN BE SET IN BODY OR TEXT AND REMAIN "BEAUTIFUL", AND FUNCTIONAL (LEGIBLE AND READABLE). MANY TYPEFACES WORK AS HEADS BUT RELATIVELY FEW FUNCTION WELL AS TEXT.

HEADLINE TYPE, OR DISPLAY TYPE, IS TYPE USED FOR NON·TEXT SOLUTIONS. MOST COMMON USES ARE AD HEADLINES, SIGNAGE, SUB·HEADS, LOGOS AND THE LIKE. THE BEST BODY TYPES MAKE EXCELLENT HEADS. IN FACT ALMOST ALL TYPE WORKS AS HEADLINE TYPE. HEADLINE SIZES ARE USUALLY MEASURED FROM A SMALL OF 14 POINT TO SIZES OF 144 POINT AND EVEN LARGER. ONLY HEADLINE TYPE SHOULD BE SET BY HAND WITH TRANSFER LETTERS. HEADLINE TYPE IS COMMONLY SET WITH PHOTO·SET MACHINES LIKE THE PHOTO· TYPOSITOR, STAROMAT, AND DIATYPE.

WHO'D WANT A MERE COPY?"

THE SAN DIEGO CHICKEN CHOKED ON A PIECE OF STYROFOAM THAT HAD BROKEN OFF HIS COSTUME.

Have lunch with a hummingbird.

BODY TYPE, ALSO KNOWN AS TEXT TYPE, IS THE SMALL TYPE WHICH CARRIES THE BULK OF THE INFORMATION IN BOOKS, MAGAZINES, NEWSPAPERS, BROCHURES, ANNUAL REPORTS, ETC. SIZE VARIES FROM 4 POINT TO 14 POINT ALTHOUGH 8, 9, 10, AND 12 POINT ARE MOST EFFECTIVE. 9 POINT IS CONSIDERED A VERY COMFORTABLE SIZE, LARGE ENOUGH TO BE READ BY OLDER EYES BUT SMALL ENOUGH TO GIVE GOOD INFORMATION DENSITY.

TEXT TYPE, LIKE HEADLINE TYPE, SHOULD BE CHOSEN FOR ITS APPROPRIATENESS. EACH TYPEFACE HAS A DISTINCT PERSONALITY. IT SHOULD ENHANCE THE MESSAGE AND STIMULATE THE AUDIENCE. RELATIVELY FEW REALLY EXCELLENT BODY TYPEFACES EXIST. THESE ARE CONSIDERED CLASSICS.

SERIF CLASSICS	SANS SERIF CLASSICS
BASKERVILLE	AVANT GARDE
BODONI	GILL
●CASLON	●HELVETICA
CENTURY	KABEL
CLARENDON	●UNIVERSE
COOPER	ANTIKVA GROTESK
GARAMOND	ERAS
GOUDY	FUTURA
MELIOR	FRANKLIN GOTHIC
●PALATINO	
OPTIMA	
●TIMES NEW ROMAN	
SOUVENIR	

SAMPLES OF BODY TYPE

The program will feature these major presentations:

Isaac Asimov on the business, financial, and social consequences of the revolution in information

Business Week International is the direct result of a worldwide commitment to meet the informational needs of its readers and the marketing needs of its

Hawaii isn't just a single island state, but eight stately islands, each with its own story. Our heri-

ART: Rudolph Hoglund (Deputy Director); Arturo Cazeneuve Ramp, William Spencer (Assistant Directors); Leonard S. L. Frank (Covers) **Layout Staff:** Burjor Nargolwala, roll Dunham, John F. Geist, Lily Hou, Modris Ramans, **Charts:** Paul J. Pugliese, Joseph Arnon, Nigel Holmes Coy, Sara Paige Noble
PHOTOGRAPHY: Arnold H. Drapkin (Picture Editor); ture Editor); Demetra Kosters (Administration) **Research** Baye, Anne Callahan, Gay Franklin, Marti Haymaker, Leverty, Julia Richer, Carol Saner, Elizabeth Statler, Walter Bennett, Sahm Doherty, Arthur Grace, Dirck Roddey E. Mims, Ralph Morse, Stephen Northup, Bill Pierce, John Zimmerman

You name it, we've got it. forests, mountain lakes and Unique resorts. Fishing, golf, back riding and more. This Central Oregon has your it! For our free booklets and maps, write:

psyche into: **Brooke Hayward,** in a four-hour CBS-TV version of *Haywire,* the bestselling daugh- ter-recall of a harrowing, hec-

TYPE

TYPE COMPOSITION ALTERNATIVES · WHEN TYPE IS ▮▮▮▮▮▮▮▮ SET IN TEXT FORM AND HEADLINE FORM, IT CAN TAKE SEVERAL SHAPES. THESE ALTERNATIVES ARE IMPORTANT TOOLS FOR THE DESIGNER. MOST OF THE SETTINGS CAN BE DONE BY MACHINE IN ADDITION TO HANDSETTING. WHEN SELECTING A COMPOSITION ALTERNATIVE, YOU SHOULD BE CAREFUL TO RESPECT THE READING PATTERNS OF THE TARGET AUDIENCE. A BOOK SHOULD NOT BE SET LIKE A POEM OR A HEADLINE. THE TYPE FUNCTION IS NOT THE SAME. VERY LITTLE WORK HAS BEEN DONE WITH ASYMMETRIC, SHAPED, AND CONCRETE SETTING. THESE ALTERNATIVES OFFER EXCITING POTENTIAL WHEN A LIMITED AMOUNT OF TYPOGRAPHIC INFORMATION IS NECESSARY.

FLUSH LEFT: RAGGED RIGHT. ▮▮▮▮▮ BEST NATURAL WORD FLOW, PREFERRED BY MOST GRAPHIC DESIGNERS. LEFT-HAND MARGIN ONLY, THE WAY A TYPEWRITER PRINTS.

Lorem ipsum dolor si incidunt ut labore nostrud exercitation duis autem vel possit duo conetud

JUSTIFIED: FLUSH LEFT AND ▮▮▮▮ RIGHT. OFTEN USED FOR BOOKS, MAGAZINES. POOR WHEN TYPE LINE IS SHORT BECAUSE OF VISUAL "HOLES" IN WORDSPACING. DIFFICULT TO CORRECT.

anim id est laborum et dolor er tempor cum soluta nobis facer possim omnis voluptas sd et aur office debit aut tum lupta recusand. Itaque earud

FLUSH RIGHT: RAGGED LEFT. ▮▮▮▮▮ VERY WEAK LEFT MARGIN RETURN FOR EYE. SUITABLE FOR SHORT INFORMATION LIKE AD COPY, BUSINESS SYSTEMS, HEADLINES. EXCELLENT WORDSPACING.

minim veniam, quis
commodo consequat. Et
molestale, vel illum
dignissium qui blandit pre
occaecat cupidiat non

CENTERED: SYMMETRICAL. ▮▮▮▮▮ BOTH LEFT AND RIGHT MARGINS ARE RAGGED. GOOD WORDSPACING. LINES SHOULD BE OF UNEQUAL LENGTH TO CREATE INTERESTING SILHOUETTE. OFTEN USED WITH SHORT COPY SUCH AS BUSINESS SYSTEMS, INVITATIONS, ANNOUNCEMENTS. VERY FORMAL.

non poest.
fautrices filelssim sed
dolor si amet, consectetur adipisci
et dolore magna aliqua
ation ullamcorper suscipit laboris

CONTOUR: TYPE FITS TO THE ▮▮▮▮▮ SHAPE OF A SYMBOL, SILHOUETTE PHOTO, OR ILLUSTRATION. COMPLEX, OFTEN COSTLY TYPESETTING. CAN GIVE FEELING OF COMFORT, EXCITEMENT. USED IN CIRCUS LAYOUT. NEEDS CONSIDERABLE COPY.

anim id est laborum et do
er tempor cum soluta no
facer possim omnis
sd et aur of
lupta recus
Lorem ipsu
incidunt ut

RUN·AROUND: TYPE WRAPS ▮▮▮▮▮ AROUND A GRAPHIC, USUALLY A SQUARED PHOTO. PICA LINE WIDTH CHANGES. USED IN BOOKS, MAGAZINES, ANNUAL REPORTS. CONSIDERABLE COPY ESSENTIAL.

luptat plenior effici
sed mult etiam ma
expetend quam no
tamet eum locum s
sic amicitiand neg posse a lupt
metus plena sit, ratiodipsa mon

ASYMMETRIC: LACKS EITHER ▮▮▮▮▮ RIGHT OR LEFT REFERENCE MARGIN. NO PREDICTABLE PATTERN OR ARRANGEMENT. GREAT VISUAL INTEREST. DIFFICULT TO READ. USE ONLY FOR SMALL AMOUNTS OF COPY. GOOD FOR BUSINESS SYSTEMS, HEADLINES, POSTERS.

memorite tum etia ergat.
conscient to factor
est neque nonor imper
Improb pary min
amititiao non modo

SHAPED: SETTING RELIES ▮▮▮▮ ON THE GESTALT IDEA OF CONTINUATION. EYE FLOWS ALONG CURVED OR IRREGULAR LINE (BASE LINE). CAN BE DONE WITH TYPE DISTORTION CAMERA OR BY HAND SETTING. EXPRESSIVE. USE ONLY FOR SMALL AMOUNTS OF COPY, AS IN BUSINESS SYSTEMS, POSTERS. QUITE RARE.

exercit no trud sei ung luptam par
disce ere cum odia solitud
in vid sunt eti am despica

CONCRETE: SETTING TAKES ▮▮▮▮▮ THE SHAPE OF AN OBJECT OR ACTION THAT IS DESCRIBED BY THE COPY. ALSO CALLED CALLIGRAMMES. EXPLORED BY FRENCH CONCRETE POETS, APOLLINAIRE, LEWIS CARROLL, E.E. CUMMINGS. ENHANCES MEANING OF TYPE. ENORMOUS POTENTIAL.

tias acce potest fie
iuda. Et tan en in busd
lar religuard cupiditat, q
it coercend magist an
tiam, aequitated ifd
sit duo conetu
but tun
g

VERTICAL TYPE · TYPE ARRANGED VERTICALLY ▬▬▬▬▬ IS OFTEN USED FOR HEADLINES, BOOK SPINES, COVERS, AND SIGNS. UNFORTUNATELY IT IS VERY OFTEN MISUSED IN THIS MANNER. BEWARE OF USING ANY LONG WORD OR HEADLINE VERTICALLY. TEXT TYPE BECOMES NEARLY IMPOSSIBLE.

T Y P E (vertical stack) ↓

TYPE (rotated) ↓

TYPE (rotated) ↓

<u>VERTICAL STACK:</u> SELDOM READABLE. UNCOMFORTABLE. LONG WORDS IMPOSSIBLE. AVOID!

<u>BOTTOM TO TOP:</u> USED FOR SIGNS. LESS READABLE THAN BOOKSPINE. POSITIVE DIRECTION.

<u>BOOKSPINE:</u> MOST READABLE. LIBRARY CONNOTATION. NEGATIVE DIRECTION.

INCLINED TYPE · TYPE SET BY ONE OF THE ▬▬▬▬▬ COMPOSITION ALTERNATIVES BUT THEN ROTATED AT AN ANGLE ON ITS FORMAT. SUCH INCLINATION CAN AFFECT THE TARGET AUDIENCE. THE DESIGNER CAN CALL ATTENTION TO A HEADLINE MESSAGE BY MOVING IT OFF THE FAMILIAR VERTICAL/HORIZONTAL AXES. INCLINED TYPE CARRIES THE ASSOCIATION OF INNOVATIVE, PROGRESSIVE, LEADING EDGE. ROTATED TYPE THAT MOVES UP AND TO THE RIGHT IS MORE COMFORTABLE THAN THAT WHICH READS DOWN TEXT TYPE CAN BE USED EFFECTIVELY IN THIS MANNER, HOWEVER IT IS DOUBTFUL THAT AN ENTIRE BOOK OR MAGAZINE WOULD BE COMFORTABLE TO READ.

Leave notes that won't get lost in the shuffle.

Power-assist front disc brakes
Hauls 1,400 pounds of cargo and
Billion-mile-proved 2-liter overhead
Torsion-bar/ball-joint front suspension
Semi-elliptical leaf springs with
Fully transistorized ignition system
Low-maintenance battery

IDENTIFICATION · TYPE IS LABELED BY DESCRIBING ▬▬▬▬▬ ITS VISUAL CHARACTERISTICS.

Gg

THIS SPECIMEN IS CALLED <u>TIMES BOLD ITALIC</u>, 60 POINT (NORMAL WIDTH)

SHAPE · <u>NAME</u> OF THE TYPEFACE, OFTEN DERIVED ▬▬▬▬▬ FROM THE NAME OF ITS DESIGNER, FROM A OBVIOUS PHYSICAL CHARACTERISTIC, OR FROM THE PURPOSE THE TYPEFACE WAS DESIGNED TO FULFILL.

SIZE · VERTICAL MEASURE OF TYPE IN <u>POINTS</u>. ▬▬▬ HEIGHT MEASURED ON CAP LETTERS.

WEIGHT · THE VISUAL WIDTH OF THE STROKES ▬▬▬▬▬ THAT BUILD EACH LETTERFORM. DESCRIPTIVE TERMS ARE <u>LIGHT</u>, <u>MEDIUM</u>, <u>BOLD</u>, <u>EXTRA BOLD</u>. THESE ARE MEASURED ON A SCALE OF BLACKNESS OR DENSITY.

WIDTH · THE HORIZONTAL MEASURE OF A TYPE ▬▬▬▬▬ CHARACTER. DESCRIPTIVE TERMS ARE <u>CONDENSED</u>, <u>NORMAL</u>, <u>EXPANDED</u> ON A VISUAL SCALE FROM NARROW TO WIDE.

SLOPE · A DESCRIPTION OF THE ANGLE OF THE ▬▬▬▬▬ AXIS OF A TYPE CHARACTER. THIS IS EITHER <u>VERTICAL</u> OR <u>ITALIC</u> (INCLINED).

TYPE SPECIMENS · THESE ARE ACCURATE SAMPLES ▬▬▬▬▬ OF HEADLINE AND BODY TYPE PRINTED ON HIGH QUALITY PAPER WITH QUALITY INK COVERAGE. SPECIMENS ARE USED FOR TRACING, SIZING AND FITTING TYPE, AND ARE ESSENTIAL FOR THE SERIOUS DESIGNER. THESE ARE THE STANDARDS FOR TYPE COMPARISON AND SPECIFICATION. SEVERAL SOURCES FOR QUALITY SPECIMENS EXIST. QUALITY TYPOGRAPHIC HOUSES ISSUE CATALOGUES TO PERMANENT CUSTOMERS. MANUFACTURERS OF PRESS-TYPE LETTERING (LETRASET) PRODUCE CATALOGUES TO PROMOTE THEIR PRODUCT. BOOKS ON TYPOGRAPHY SOMETIMES INCLUDE GOOD SPECIMENS. LARGE PRINTERS, UNIVERSITIES, AND PRIVATE PRESSES OFTEN HAVE IN-HOUSE SPECIMENS. FOR MORE LIMITED SAMPLES, NEWSPAPERS AND MAGAZINES SHOULD NOT BE OVERLOOKED.

TYPE

- A FUNDAMENTAL CONCEPT EXISTS FOR SOLVING TYPOGRAPHIC PROBLEMS, THE CONCEPT OF OBVIOUS CONTRAST. WE MUST COMPARE TWO OPPOSITE VISUAL EFFECTS TO MAKE THE CONCEPT CLEAR TO A TARGET AUDIENCE. CONTRAST IS A DYNAMIC POLARITY THAT HELPS TO CLARIFY A GRAPHIC IDEA. CONTRAST IS A FORCE OF VISUAL INTENSITY AND AS SUCH IT SIMPLIFIES THE PROCESS OF COMMUNICATION.
- WHEN SELECTING TYPE TO CONVEY AN IDEA WE MUST BE CAREFUL TO LIMIT OUR CHOICES. OFTEN A SINGLE TYPEFACE IN A SINGLE SIZE IS ENOUGH TO SOLVE A PROBLEM EFFECTIVELY. MORE THAN TWO TYPEFACES CAN MUDDY THE WATER OF OBVIOUS CONTRAST. THE AUDIENCE MUST QUICKLY BE ABLE TO IDENTIFY TYPOGRAPHIC CONTRAST OR THE INTENSITY OF THE VISUAL MESSAGE WILL BE LOST. EXAGGERATION IS EFFECTIVE.

SMALL · LARGE · CONTRAST HERE IS SIZE. BIG TO LITTLE. SCALE (SIZE COMPARISON WITH FAMILIAR SIZE TYPE) ALSO PLAYS A ROLE.

THICK · THIN · CONTRAST IS WEIGHT. LIGHT TO HEAVY. BLACK TO GREY. STRONG TO WEAK.

HARD · SOFT · CONTRAST IS IN A SENSE TACTILE. WE "FEEL" THE TYPE SHAPES, EDGES.

NARROW · WIDE · CONTRAST IS A HORIZONTAL MEASURE. CLOSED TO OPEN. NARROW TO WIDE. TIGHT TO LOOSE.

VERTICAL · INCLINED · CONTRAST IS STABLE TO DYNAMIC, PERPENDICULAR TO ANGULAR, STOP TO GO.

SOLID · OUTLINE · CONTRAST IS FULL TO EMPTY, POSITIVE TO NEGATIVE, OFF TO ON, BLACK TO WHITE, YES TO NO.

SOLID · FRAGMENTED · CONTRAST IS WHOLE TO PARTS, COMPLETE TO INCOMPLETE, TRANQUILITY TO DISRUPTION.

- IF, WHEN DESIGNING WITH TYPE, YOU EXPLORE ONE OF THESE SEVEN CONTRASTS WITH A DIRECTNESS AND A CONCERN FOR FUNCTION YOU WILL HAVE A GOOD CHANCE FOR EFFECTIVENESS. IF YOU MIX THE CONTRASTS BE PREPARED FOR PROBLEMS. MAKE ONE OF THE CONTRASTS YOUR "BIG IDEA", DEVELOP ALTERNATIVES, AND A VALID SOLUTION WILL COME YOUR WAY.

READABILITY · THE EASE OF READING A PRINTED PAGE OR MESSAGE. IT REFERS TO THE ARRANGEMENT OF TYPE(S). READABILITY INVOLVES DESIGN OF THE TOTAL VISUAL ENTITY, THE COMPLEX INTERRELATIONSHIPS AMONG TYPE, SYMBOLS, PHOTOS, AND ILLUSTRATIONS.

LEGIBILITY · IS CONCERNED WITH TYPE DESIGN, THE VISUAL SHAPE OF INDIVIDUAL TYPE CHARACTERS. LEGIBILITY IS THE SPEED WITH WHICH A TYPE CHARACTER CAN BE IDENTIFIED. MANY TIMES TESTING INVOLVES QUICKLY FLASHING THE CHARACTER(S) TO DETERMINE THE TIME OF AUDIENCE RECOGNITION. LEGIBILITY IS PARTICULARLY IMPORTANT WHEN DESIGNING SIGNS, PACKAGING, LOGOS, BILLBOARDS, AND VEHICLE GRAPHICS.

SOME VALUABLE TYPOGRAPHIC HINTS

■ 9,10,11,12 POINT ARE BEST FOR TEXT TYPE MATTER. USE 11, 12 POINT WHEN TYPEFACE HAS A SMALL X·HEIGHT (CENTURY). USE 9,10 POINT WHEN TYPEFACE HAS LARGE X·HEIGHT (HELVETICA).

■ FOR 9,10,11,12 POINT TYPE, A LINE WIDTH BETWEEN 18-24 PICAS (ABOUT 10-12 WORDS PER LINE) IS MOST READABLE.

■ BEWARE OF NO LINESPACING (TYPE SET SOLID). ALL TYPEFACES ARE MORE READABLE WITH MODERATE LEADING THAN WITH NONE AT ALL. LINESPACING NORMALLY VARIES FROM 1 TO 4 POINTS. HEAVY FACES SHOULD HAVE MORE LEADING. LONG LINES NEED MORE LEADING.

■ MEDIUM WEIGHT TEXT IS MORE READABLE THAN VERY LIGHT OR VERY BOLD TEXT. BOLD WEIGHT TEXT IS SUPERIOR TO ITALICS FOR EMPHASIS - BUT IT MUST BE USED IN MODERATION TO AVOID TIRING THE EYE.

■ SERIF FACES ARE SLIGHTLY MORE LEGIBLE THAN SANS·SERIF FACES. SERIF FACES ARE PREFERRED OVER SANS·SERIF FACES BY READERS.

■ UNJUSTIFIED TYPESETTING HAS SEVERAL ADVANTAGES OVER JUSTIFIED TYPESETTING. IT REDUCES PRODUCTION COSTS, MAKES CORRECTIONS EASIER, AND AIDS READABILITY BY LETTING THE EYE RELAX WITH A SINGLE REFERENCE MARGIN.

■ ALL·CAPS TYPESETTINGS REDUCE READING SPEED BY ABOUT 15%.

■ PARAGRAPH INDENTS MUST BE SUBSTANTIAL (NEVER LESS THAN ONE EM) OR TYPE MARGINS WILL APPEAR TO CURVE. EXTRA LINESPACING MAY BE SUBSTITUTED FOR INDENTS.

■ CONSIDER ELIMINATING "WIDOWS" BY EDITING. WIDOWS ARE ENDING LINES OF TYPE WITH ONLY A SINGLE WORD IN THE LINE.

■ HEADLINES WITH NORMAL (UPPER AND LOWER CASE) TYPESETTING ARE EASIER TO READ THAN THOSE SET IN ALL UPPER OR ALL LOWER CASE. CONSIDER BREAKING HEADLINES INTO READING PHRASES, TO REFLECT PHONICS (WORD SOUNDS, EMPHASES).

● FOR TELEVISION TYPOGRAPHY, MEDIUM WEIGHT SANS·SERIF AND THICK SERIF FACES ARE BEST. BEWARE OF THE SERIF FACES WITH EXTREME THICK·THIN CONTRAST. FINE LINE SCRIPT FACES AND TEXT FACES ARE USUALLY UNSATISFACTORY FOR THE MEDIUM ALSO. TELEVISION PICTURES ARE CREATED BY SCANNING BEAMS WHICH DO NOT EFFECTIVELY CAPTURE EXTREMELY FINE SERIFS, LINES, OR DETAILS. TYPE FILLS IN EASILY, SHARP CORNERS TEND TO ROUND, DETAIL EVEN DISAPPEARS. IT IS WISE TO TEST A MARGINAL TYPEFACE BY VIEWING IT ON A MONITOR BEFORE FINISHING PRODUCTION.

● FOR OUTDOOR TYPOGRAPHY, BOLD IS BEST SIMPLY BECAUSE IT NEEDS TO BE SEEN IN A HURRY. LEGIBILITY IS EXTREMELY IMPORTANT. READABILITY IS CRUCIAL ALTHOUGH A BILLBOARD SHOULD HAVE PREFERABLY FEWER THAN SEVEN WORDS. AVOID ELABORATE SCRIPTS AND TEXT FACES. FIGURE THREE INCHES OF HEIGHT FOR EACH 100 FEET OF VIEWING DISTANCE. BEWARE OF ALL·CAPS SETTINGS UNLESS THE MESSAGE IS A SINGLE WORD. THE TYPOGRAPHIC CLASSICS MAKE EFFECTIVE CHOICES WHEN USED IN THEIR BOLDER VERSIONS.

GIANTS OF TYPOGRAPHY

HERBERT BAYER	PAUL RAND
JAN TSCHICHOLD	ALAN PECKOLICK
HERB LUBALIN	GEORGE TSCHERNY
AARON BURNS	ADRIAN FRUTIGER
WOLFGANG WEINGART	ARMIN HOFFMAN
BRADBURY THOMPSON	IVAN CHERMAYEFF
MILTON GLASER	FRITZ GOTTSHALK
HERMAN ZAPF	MASSIMO VIGNELLI

● "A WORK OF TYPOGRAPHY MUST NOT ONLY BE SUITABLE FOR ITS PURPOSE AND EASY TO PRODUCE, BUT ALSO BEAUTIFUL."   ● JAN TSCHICHOLD

● "DISPUTES ARISING BETWEEN THE TWO SCHOOLS OF TYPOGRAPHIC THOUGHT, THE TRADITIONAL.... AND THE MODERN, ARE, IT SEEMS TO ME THE FRUITS OF MISPLACED EMPHASIS. I BELIEVE THE REAL DIFFERENCE LIES IN THE WAY 'SPACE' IS INTERPRETED."
   ● PAUL RAND

TYPE

TO SET HEADLINE TYPE

<u>PRESS TYPE</u>·TRANSFER LETTERS

<u>HAND SET</u>·FROM TYPE CASE, LETTERPRESS, PROOF

<u>STAR·O·MAT</u>·LINEAR SINGLE CHARACTER HEADLINER

<u>PHOTOTYPOSITOR</u>·MOST FLEXIBLE SINGLE CHARACTER HEADLINER, DISTORTS, CURVES, ALLOWS GREAT TYPOGRAPHIC CREATIVITY. SLOW.

<u>DIATYPE</u>· SEMI·AUTOMATIC SINGLE CHARACTER HEADLINER, MASTER LETTERS ON METAL DISC, CAPABLE OF EXTREMELY HIGH QUALITY.

<u>COMPUTER HEADLINER</u> · KEYBOARD CHARACTER GENERATION, COMPUGRAPHIC, VARITYPER, ETC. FAST, CAPABLE OF MANY SIZES. IN WIDE USE.

TO SET TEXT TYPE

<u>HAND SET</u>· FROM TYPE CASE, PROOF BY LETTERPRESS MOVABLE TYPE, SAME AS GUTENBERG (1440)

<u>LINOTYPE, INTERTYPE</u>· HOT TYPE, CAST ENTIRE LINES OF TYPE BY KEYBOARD. NEARLY OBSOLETE.

<u>MONOTYPE</u>· HOT METAL, CASTS INDIVIDUAL LETTERS BY KEYBOARD. SLOW. NEARLY OBSOLETE.

<u>TYPEWRITER</u>· KEYBOARD, LETTERS STRUCK ON. VERY FAST. IBM BEST KNOWN. ALLOWS EDITING, CORRECTIONS. LIMITED LETTERSPACING, FONT MIX.

<u>PHOTO·OPTIC</u> · COMPUTER CONTROLLED, KEYBOARD(S) VERY FAST, SHARP, PRECISE LETTERSPACING. FAR AND AWAY THE DOMINANT TYPESETTING IN THE U.S. TODAY. TYPE ON PAPER, FILM.

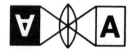

Light Source · Optical Negative · Lens · Film or Paper

<u>PHOTO·SCAN</u> · FASTEST SYSTEM, CRT SCAN, COMPUTER CONTROLLED, EXPENSIVE, CAN SET ENTIRE PAGES IN POSITION, TYPE ON PAPER, FILM.

Optical Negative · Image Pick-up · Digital Image · CRT Scan · Lens · Film or Paper

<u>SELECTING TYPESETTING</u> · THIS CAN POSE SOME MINOR PROBLEMS. THESE RELATE TO TYPE QUALITY, DEGREE OF LETTERSPACING FLEXIBILITY, AND SERVICE. ALL OF THESE FACTORS CONTRIBUTE TO PRICE, AND WITH TYPESETTING YOU GET WHAT YOU PAY FOR. THE MOST SOPHISTICATED LETTERSPACING IS GENERATED BY COMPUTER, WITH EXTREMELY COMPLEX PROGRAMMING. SUCH TEXT TYPE IS EXPENSIVE BUT IS VISUALLY SUPERIOR. TYPE QUALITY IS RELATED TO MACHINE FILM MASTERS AND OPTICS. THE BEST TYPE SHOULD HAVE PRECISE EDGES, BE OF A CONSISTENT VISUAL DENSITY, AND BE CAPABLE OF EXTENSIVE PHOTO ENLARGEMENT. SERVICE IS CRITICAL WITH TYPESETTING. DESIGN DEMANDS QUICK TURNAROUND. TYPE MUST COME TO THE DESIGNER TO MEET PASTE·UP DEADLINES WITHOUT THE NEED FOR EXTENSIVE CORRECTIONS.

MANUSCRIPT

<u>INPUT</u> KEYBOARD·EDIT

STORAGE COMPUTER PHOTO·OPTIC PRINTER

<u>OUTPUT</u> TYPE GALLEYS ON FILM, PAPER TO PASTE·UP

<u>THE TYPE·SETTING PROCESS</u> · THE ABOVE DIAGRAM SHOWS HOW MOST TYPESETTING IS DONE TODAY. TWO PHASES TO REMEMBER ARE INPUT AND OUTPUT. INPUT INVOLVES KEYBOARDING INFORMATION INTO A RECORDER (COMPUTER), AND ASSIGNING IT A CODE (TYPE FACE, SIZE, LINE LENGTH, LINESPACING, ETC.) OUTPUT INVOLVES ACTUALLY CREATING THE TYPE THROUGH OPTICS AND PHOTO PROCESS AND MAKING IT READY TO BE PASTED UP FOR CAMERA·READY ART. MANY VARIATIONS EXIST AT EACH STAGE OF THE PROCESS AS THE STATE OF THE ART IS IN RAPID CHANGE.

COPY PREPARATION

PROPER PREPARATION OF COPY FOR TYPESETTING IS ESSENTIAL. SINCE TYPESETTING IS BILLED BY TIME, "CLEAN" COPY WILL BE EASIER FOR THE TYPESETTER TO READ AND THEREBY COST LESS. "CLEAN" MANUSCRIPTS MINIMIZE TYPESETTING ERRORS. THE GOAL SHOULD BE TO PASS ON TO THE TYPESETTER A PERFECT MANUSCRIPT, WITH CORRECT SPELLING, CLEAR MARK·UP AND PLENTY OF ROOM FOR ADDITIONAL TYPESETTER MARKS.

PAPER · USE BRIGHT WHITE 8½"X 11" BOND OR ERASABLE BOND. SOME TYPE HOUSES PROVIDE A SPECIAL PRE·PRINTED MANUSCRIPT PAPER WITH PROPER MARGINS, ETC.

COPY FORMAT · COPY SHOULD BE TYPED ON ONE SIDE OF THE SHEET ONLY. LINES OF TYPING SHOULD BE DOUBLE SPACED, FLUSH· LEFT. COLUMN WIDTH SHOULD BE ABOUT 6," EACH LINE HAVING ABOUT THE SAME NUMBER OF CHARACTERS. EACH PAGE OF THE MANUSCRIPT SHOULD HAVE ABOUT THE SAME NUMBER OF LINES.

● LOTS OF SPACE ON THE LEFT MARGIN
DEEP TOP MARGIN

● DOUBLE SPACE TYPEWRITER LINES
(4 SPACES FOR PARAGRAPH)

● ABOUT 6" TYPEWRITER COLUMN WIDTH
● FLUSH LEFT MARGIN (ABOUT 2" WIDE)

PAGE IDENTITY · EACH PAGE OF THE MANUSCRIPT NEEDS IDENTIFICATION IN CASE IT IS LOST OR MISPLACED. EACH PAGE SHOULD INCLUDE FIRM NAME/YOUR NAME AND THE CLIENT. EACH PAGE SHOULD BE NUMBERED. LAST PAGE SHOULD SAY "END."

● PAGE NUMBER HERE OR IN UPPER RIGHT CORNER

● CLIENT / YOUR NAME
(EXAMPLE : ARTGLASS AD / DESIGN +)

MARK·UP · INVOLVES YOU TELLING THE TYPESETTER PRECISELY HOW YOU WANT YOUR TYPE TO LOOK WHEN IT IS SET. MARK·UP INCLUDES A CAREFULLY WRITTEN SET OF INSTRUCTIONS PLACED PROPERLY ON THE MANUSCRIPT. MAKE SURE ALL YOUR INSTRUCTIONS ARE CLEAR...WHAT IS CLEAR TO YOU MIGHT NOT BE CLEAR TO ANOTHER PERSON. MARK UP SHOULD BE DONE IN PEN. A COLOR LIKE RED OR BLUE GIVES GOOD CONTRAST. DO MARK·UP ON THE ORIGINAL MANUSCRIPT BUT XEROX A COPY OF THE MANUSCRIPT IN CASE IT GETS LOST IN THE MAIL. ANY CORRECTIONS IN THE MANUSCRIPT SHOULD BE WRITTEN ABOVE TYPEWRITER LINES.

● ALL MARK·UP SHOULD BE DONE IN THE WIDE LEFT MARGIN

● ALL CORRECTIONS SHOULD BE WRITTEN ABOVE THE TYPEWRITER LINES

MARK·UP MUST CALL OUT THE TYPE FACE, SIZE, PICA LINE LENGTH, COMPOSITION SYSTEM, CAPITALIZATION, LINESPACING, PARAGRAPH SPACING, AND INDENTATION.

SAMPLE MANUSCRIPT MARK·UP

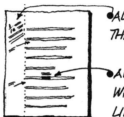

10	The Centre de Créa
HELVETICA LITE	
U/LC	ted an internation
22 PICA LINE	
FLUSH LEFT/ [	Centre National d'
RAG RIGHT	
10/12	The main objective
S.L. 1 LINE SP	We are particularly
NO INDENT	mation as possible

■ THESE INSTRUCTIONS TELL THE TYPESETTER TO SET THE MANUSCRIPT IN 10 POINT HELVETICA LITE TYPE WITH NORMAL UPPER AND LOWER AS SHOWN. THE TYPE WILL BE SET ON A 22 PICA LONG LINE WITH A FLUSH LEFT MARGIN AND A RAGGED RIGHT MARGIN. LINESPACING WILL BE TWO POINTS (10/12). THERE WILL BE NO INDENTATIONS AND EACH OF THE PARAGRAPHS WILL BE ONE FULL LINESPACE APART.
● THESE UNIVERSAL SPECS PROVIDE CAMERA·READY GALLEYS.

STAGES

THE DESIGN/REPRODUCTION PROCESS NORMALLY PROGRESSES THROUGH A SERIES OF DISTINCT STAGES OR STEPS. THERE ARE SITUATIONS WHERE SEQUENCE VARIES SLIGHTLY, OR A STAGE IS OMITTED.

1 RESEARCH · AFTER A VISUAL PROBLEM HAS BEEN POSED, THE DESIGNER NEEDS TO DEVELOP A PROGRAM FOR ATTACKING THE PROBLEM. APPROPRIATE RESEARCH STARTS HERE. AUDIENCE, FORMATS, BUDGETS, AND TIME CONSTRAINTS ARE EXAMINED. PERHAPS A BRIEF OR PROPOSAL IS PREPARED IN WRITTEN FORM, RE-DEFINING THE PROBLEM BASED ON LITERATURE AND MARKET SEARCHES. A PRELIMINARY IDEA OF INDIVIDUAL OR TEAM APPROACH IS FORMULATED. THIS MIGHT BE THE MOST SIGNIFICANT STAGE IN THE ENTIRE PROCESS BECAUSE EFFECTIVE RESEARCH WILL OFTEN NEARLY SOLVE THE PROBLEM. SOLID RESEARCH REDUCES DESIGN TIME AND SERVES TO FOCUS ON THE ESSENCE OF A VISUAL PROBLEM.

2 THUMBNAILS · THESE PRELIMINARY IDEA SKETCHES ARE THE FIRST TRANSLATION OF RESEARCH INTO VISUAL FORM. WHEN DESIGNERS DO THUMBNAILS, THEY "THINK WITH THEIR PENCILS." THUMBNAILS ALLOW DESIGNERS TO EXPLORE ALTERNATIVE CONCEPTS, AND COMPARE THEM. THESE SKETCHES ARE ONLY FOR THE DESIGNER AND ART DIRECTOR, NOT FOR THE CLIENT. SMALL, FAST, AND APPROXIMATE, THUMBNAILS DO NOT ALLOW DETAIL TO GET IN THE WAY OF SOLID "BIG IDEAS." EFFECTIVE THUMBNAIL TECHNIQUE COMES WITH PRACTICE.....ITS IMPOSSIBLE TO GET TOO FAST OR TOO PROLIFIC. THE BEST DESIGNERS DO THE BEST AND FASTEST THUMBNAILS.

3 ROUGHS · THESE ARE "REFINED THUMBNAILS", LARGER AND MORE DETAILED, WITH TYPE ROUGHED IN POSITION. THE PRIMARY PURPOSE OF ROUGHS IS TO MORE CLOSELY EXAMINE PROMISING THUMBNAILS BY TESTING COLOR, TYPE, AND ILLUSTRATIVE ALTERNATIVES. ROUGHS ARE NOT TO BE SEEN BY THE CLIENT. THEY ARE USED TO PREDICT AND TEST WHETHER A "BIG IDEA" IS FEASIBLE. SOMETIMES ROUGHS ARE OMITTED FROM THE DESIGN PROCESS. OCCASIONALLY SKETCHES WILL BE HYBRIDS, VERY DIFFICULT TO CLASSIFY. MANY THREE-DIMENSIONAL ROUGHS ARE USED TO CHECK SHAPES OF PACKAGES, SIGNS, AND EXHIBITS.

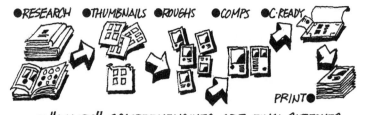

●RESEARCH ●THUMBNAILS ●ROUGHS ●COMPS ●C. READY PRINT●

4 "COMPS". COMPREHENSIVES ARE FINAL SKETCHES OR MODELS AND ARE PRESENTED TO THE CLIENT. FROM THEM THE CLIENT MAKES A "YES" OR "NO" DECISION. IF "NO," MORE COMPS ARE PRESENTED UNTIL THE CLIENT IS SATISFIED. IF "YES," THE PROCESS CONTINUES. THE COMP IS A HIGHLY FINISHED MOCK-UP OR MODEL OF A PRINTED PIECE THAT ATTEMPTS TO DUPLICATE IN VISUAL APPEARANCE THE FINISHED PRODUCT. DEPENDING ON BUDGET AND TIME CONSTRAINTS, THE COMP MIGHT INCLUDE COLOR KEYS, PRESS TYPE, PMT STATS, MACHINE SET TYPE, CUT FILM, PMS PAPER, PHOTO PRINTS, VERY TIGHT RENDERINGS OR ILLUSTRATIONS, SCREEN PRINTING, ETC. LEAVE NO STONE UNTURNED TO POLISH THE COMP. WHEN THE CHIPS ARE DOWN ITS JUST YOU, YOUR CLIENT, AND YOUR COMP. IN MOST SITUATIONS ALTERNATIVE COMPS ARE PRESENTED TO GIVE THE CLIENT A CHOICE. YOUR COMPS SHOULD CLEARLY REFLECT YOUR TWO OR THREE BEST "BIG IDEAS." IF YOU ARE PRESENTING AN AD, SHOW IT IN THE MAGAZINE IN WHICH IT WILL APPEAR. IF A PACKAGE, SHOW IT WITH THE PACKAGES OF A STRONG COMPETITOR. SIMULATE THE IN-USE SITUATION.

5 CAMERA-READY ART · AFTER THE COMP HAS BEEN APPROVED IT MUST BE CONVERTED INTO BLACK AND WHITE ART FOR REPRODUCTION. THIS CAMERA-READY ART, ALSO KNOWN AS LAYOUT ART OR MECHANICAL ART, IS EXTREMELY PRECISE AND CARRIES SPECIFICATIONS FOR PRINTING. IT BECOMES THE PROPERTY OF THE CLIENT, BUT IS SHOWN TO THE CLIENT ONLY IN PROOF FORM FOR FINAL SIGNATURE APPROVAL. IT IS USUALLY STORED WITH THE DESIGN FIRM FOR CONVENIENCE.

6 PRINTED PIECES · THESE ARE THE GOAL OF THE ENTIRE EFFORT... WHAT THE CLIENT WILL USE AS A TOOL FOR PERSUASION AND SALES. OFTEN PROOFED BEFORE FINAL PRINTING, THIS PRODUCT MUST BE CAREFULLY QUALITY-CONTROLLED TO INSURE FIDELITY OF CONCEPT. DELIVERED IN PROPER QUANTITY AND ON TIME WITHIN BUDGET, PRINTED PIECES MARK THE LAST STAGE IN THE DESIGN PROCESS. DESIGNERS SHOULD COLLECT SAMPLES FOR PORTFOLIO.

THUMBNAILS

THE ABILITY TO DO THUMBNAILS IS FUNDAMENTAL TO TRANSFORMING MENTAL IDEAS INTO VISUAL FORM. IDEA SKETCHES ARE NECESSARY FOR ANY DESIGN ACTIVITY. DOING THUMBNAILS WELL DOES NOT REQUIRE REALISTIC FREEHAND DRAWING TECHNIQUES. IT DOES REQUIRE PRECISION AND A DRIVE TO MAKE EACH SKETCH BETTER THAN THE ONE BEFORE IT. A DESIGNER CAN NEVER DO TOO MANY THUMBNAILS, AS THEY CHART A PATH OF "VISUAL THINKING" IN THE DESIGN PROCESS.

CHARACTERISTICS · THUMBNAILS ARE SMALL IN SIZE ███████ BUT PROPORTIONAL. IF THE PROBLEM IS A POSTER, A GOOD THUMBNAIL SIZE IS $1\frac{1}{2}"\times 2"$, A SIZE IN DIRECT PROPORTION TO AN $18"\times 24"$ PRINTED POSTER. FOR A RECORD COVER A GOOD SIZE IS $2"\times 2"$, IN DIRECT PROPORTION TO THE $12\frac{1}{4}"\times 12\frac{1}{4}"$ SQUARE FORMAT OF THE PACKAGE. WE ALWAYS WANT TO PICK A SIZE PROPORTIONAL TO THE PRINTED PIECE, YET CONVENIENT TO OUR PENCIL, PEN, MARKERS, AND MONTAGE MATERIALS.

■ THUMBNAILS ARE SMALL BECAUSE SMALL IS FAST. A QUALITY THUMBNAIL SHOULD TAKE NO LONGER THAN A FEW MINUTES TO FINISH (IN COLOR). PRODUCE LOTS OF SKETCHES IN A SHORT TIME. EXPLORE A WIDE VARIETY OF IDEAS. EMPTY YOUR BRAIN. NEVER REJECT AN IDEA UNTIL YOU TEST IT WITH A SKETCH. SMALL SCALE HAS ANOTHER BIG ADVANTAGE. DETAIL IN TYPE AND IMAGE IS LIMITED.

■ ITS A GOOD IDEA TO ORGANIZE THUMBNAILS ON YOUR PAPER (LAYOUT PAPER, RAG BOND, AND TISSUE ARE OK). SPREAD THEM OUT. CROWDING ON THE SHEET WILL MAKE THEM HARD TO EVALUATE. SAVE AND FILE YOUR SKETCHES; THEY MAY BE VALUABLE IN THE FUTURE.

A TECHNIQUE · EXPERIENCED DESIGNERS DEVELOP ███████ THEIR INDIVIDUAL TECHNIQUES AND MEDIA PREFERENCES. THE FOLLOWING SUGGESTIONS WILL LEAD TO CLEAN COMMUNICATIVE THUMBNAILS.

MEASURE AND DRAW A BLANK MASTER. USE TOOLS, DARK LINE.

TRACE THUMBNAIL BORDERS FROM THE MASTER WITH PENCIL. KEEP SPREAD OUT! SKETCH.

● TRACE THE SKETCH BORDER WITH #2 PENCIL. USE A VARIABLE WEIGHT LINE WITH MORE WEIGHT OR EMPHASIS AT THE CORNERS.

THESE THUMBNAILS INDICATE POSTER IDEAS. THUMBNAILS MUST HAVE TYPE INDICATION ABOUT THE LENGTH THE FINAL PIECE WILL REQUIRE.

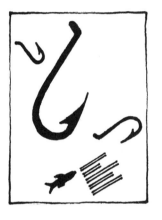

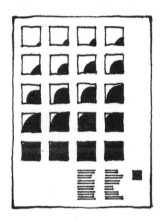

■ THUMBNAILS ARE VALUABLE FOR SHOWING RELATIONSHIPS AMONG TYPE, SYMBOLS, AND ILLUSTRATIVE MATTER. THEY ALLOW QUICK TESTING OF ALTERNATIVE TYPE COMPOSITION SYSTEMS. THEY ENCOURAGE COLOR ALTERNATIVES. EFFECTIVE THUMBNAILS CAN ALSO BE DONE BY THE USE OF EXISTING SUGGESTIVE PHOTO IMAGES CUT FROM PUBLICATIONS AND GLUED IN POSITION.

COLOR

col·or (kul'ẽr), *n.* [ME. *color, colour*; OFr. *colour*; L. *color*; OL. *colos,* orig., a covering < *celare,* to cover, hide], 1. the sensation resulting from stimulation of the retina of the eye by light waves of certain lengths. 2. the property of reflecting light waves of a particular length: the *primary colors* of the spectrum are red, orange, yellow, green, blue, indigo, and violet. •

■ COLOR • THE WAY AN OBJECT ABSORBS OR REFLECTS LIGHT.

■ COLOR • THE KIND OF LIGHT THAT STRIKES AN OBJECT.

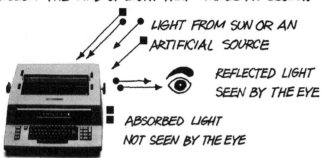

LIGHT FROM SUN OR AN ARTIFICIAL SOURCE

REFLECTED LIGHT SEEN BY THE EYE

ABSORBED LIGHT NOT SEEN BY THE EYE

SPECTRUM • VISIBLE RANGE OF COLORS. NEWTON PASSED WHITE LIGHT THROUGH A PRISM AND DISCOVERED A RANGE OF HUES OR COLOR SAMPLES.

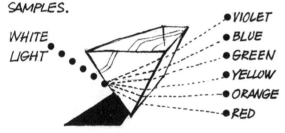

WHITE LIGHT

• VIOLET
• BLUE
• GREEN
• YELLOW
• ORANGE
• RED

■ WE SEE A SIMILAR HAPPENING WHEN WE EXPERIENCE A RAINBOW IN NATURE, LIGHT BROKEN INTO A SPECTRUM. WE SEE NO CLEAR BORDER BUT A SMOOTH TRANSITION OF COLOR BANDS. IF WE THINK OF THE RAINBOW AS A THREE DIMENSIONAL TUBE AND CUT IT OPEN AND TURN IT ON END, WE CAN VISUALIZE A "COLOR WHEEL"

■ THE DESIGNER MIXING PAINTS SEES COLOR ONE WAY. WHITENESS BECOMES THE LACK OF COLOR WHILE BLACK BECOMES THE SUM OF ALL COLORS. PHYSICISTS SEE COLOR DIFFERENTLY... AS THEY DEAL WITH LIGHT BLACK IS THE TOTAL ABSENCE OF COLOR, WHITE IS THE PRESENCE OF ALL COLORS. AS DESIGNERS WE SHOULD KNOW COLOR THOROUGHLY FROM THE MIXING VIEWPOINT. PAINT MIXING SYSTEMS, INK MIXING SYSTEMS, THE COLORS OF PAPER, AND

COLOR WE PERCEIVE IN WORKING WITH COLOR TRANSPARENCIES SHOULD BE THE FOCUS OF OUR STUDY OF COLOR. EVEN WHEN DESIGNING FOR FILM AND TELEVISION, WE SHOULD FOCUS ON COLOR MIXING. DO NOT CONFUSE THE PHYSICS OF LIGHT IN THE TELEVISION SYSTEM WITH THE PREPARATION OF GRAPHICS FOR THE SYSTEM. PERHAPS MORE IMPORTANT TO THE DESIGNER IS THE REACTION OF HIS TARGET AUDIENCE TO A COLOR SAMPLE. THIS IS THE PSYCHOLOGY OF COLOR SENSATION, AND INVOLVES MAKING A COLOR CHOICE TO STIMULATE AN AUDIENCE.

A • COLOR IN LIGHT • COLOR AS IN PHYSICS. LIGHT COMPRISED OF COLOR. COLOR AS IN THE TELEVISION SYSTEM, COLOR AS IN THE COLOR PHOTOGRAPHY PROCESS. WHITE IS SUM OF ALL COLORS. BLACK IS ABSENCE OF ALL COLORS.

B COLOR PIGMENT • COLOR IN PAINT, INK, PAPERS PRINTING SEPARATIONS, COLOR KEYS. WHITE IS LACK OF COLORS. BLACK IS SUM OF ALL COLORS. OF GREAT INTEREST TO GRAPHIC DESIGNERS. MANY CLASSIFICATION SYSTEMS (OSTWALD ETC.)

C COLOR SENSATION • AS PSYCHOLOGY. HOW AUDIENCES REACT TO SPECIFIC COLOR SAMPLES. ASSOCIATIONS, CONNOTATIONS, PREFERENCES . CRITICAL FOR GRAPHIC DESIGNER.

COLOR DIMENSION • INVOLVES DESCRIBING A COLOR SAMPLE. DESIGNERS SHOULD BE SENSITIVE TO COLOR, BE ABLE TO CLASSIFY COLOR, AND BE ABLE TO SPECIFY COLOR. THE USE OF THE FOLLOWING TERMS WILL HELP YOU BE SPECIFIC AND AID YOUR COMMUNICATION WITH DESIGNERS, PRINTERS, CLIENTS, AND SUPPLIERS.

HUE • NAME FOR A COLOR SAMPLE. THE TERM WHICH DISTINGUISHES ONE COLOR SAMPLE FROM ANOTHER. AN EXAMPLE WOULD BE ORANGE BUT THE SAMPLE DOES NOT HAVE TO BE PURE ORANGE, ONLY ABLE TO BE DETERMINED AS "AN ORANGE SAMPLE." THERE ARE THOUSANDS OF HUES YET THE AVERAGE PERSON HAS A FAMILIARITY WITH AND CAN ONLY NAME 18 TO 20. THE NAMABLE HUES ARE THE MOST MEMORABLE, SELL MERCHANDISE BEST, AND ARE THE MOST EFFECTIVE DESIGN CHOICES.

VALUE · LIGHTNESS OR DARKNESS OF A COLOR SAMPLE. ▮ A LIGHT OR DARK VARIATION OF A HUE. WHITE PLUS A PURE HUE GIVES A LIGHT VALUE OR A TINT. BLACK PLUS A PURE HUE GIVES A DARK VALUE OR A SHADE. A TINT OF RED WOULD BE PINK WHILE A SHADE OF RED WOULD BE MAROON.

CHROMA · SATURATION OR INTENSITY OF A COLOR ▮ SAMPLE. THE BRIGHTNESS OR DULLNESS OF A COLOR SAMPLE. STRONG CHROMA SAMPLES APPROACH A PURE HUE. WEAK CHROMA SAMPLES APPROACH A NEUTRAL GREY. THE AMOUNT OF PURE HUE IN A COLOR SAMPLE. HIGHLY SATURATED HUES ARE MORE EASILY NAMABLE, MEMORABLE, AND GENERALLY MORE EFFECTIVE FOR SELLING.

SURFACE · THE SAME HUE LOOKS DIFFERENT WHEN ▮ APPLIED TO DIFFERENT SURFACES. SURFACES SUCH AS AUTOMOTIVE BODIES ARE EXTREMELY HARD AND SMOOTH. A HUE ON THAT SURFACE APPEARS GLOSSY. ON AN ABSORBENT SURFACE LIKE UNCOATED PAPER, THE SAME HUE WOULD APPEAR MATTE OR DULL. SURFACE QUALITY AFFECTS HOW AN AUDIENCE RESPONDS TO A VISUAL MESSAGE AND A TACTILE MESSAGE.

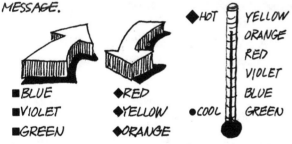

◆HOT
YELLOW
ORANGE
RED
VIOLET
BLUE
●COOL GREEN

■BLUE ◆RED
■VIOLET ◆YELLOW
■GREEN ◆ORANGE

ADVANCE · RECEDE · HUES WITH SHORT WAVE LENGTHS ▮ APPEAR TO MOVE BACK FROM THE EYE. LONG WAVE LENGTH HUES APPEAR TO ADVANCE TOWARDS THE EYE. THE COOL HUES RECEDE. THE WARM HUES ADVANCE. THIS PHENOMENON CAN EXPLAIN WHY COLOR AFFECTS THE APPARENT SIZES OF CLOTHING, ROOMS, PACKAGES, AND VEHICLES.

VISIBILITY · COLORS THAT ARE VISIBLE AT THE ▮ GREATEST DISTANCE WILL ALSO ATTRACT THE EYE THE QUICKEST, EVEN AT SHORT RANGE. PURE HUES ARE MORE VISIBLE THAN THEIR TINTS, SHADES AND TONES. VISIBILITY OF COLOR COMBINATIONS IS DETERMINED BY CONTRAST.... THE MORE CONTRAST, THE MORE VISIBILITY. HIGHEST VISIBILITY PAIRS ARE BLACK/YELLOW, BLACK/WHITE, BLUE/WHITE AND GREEN/WHITE. "REVERSE" PAIRS LOOK ABOUT 10% LARGER.

ENVIRONMENT · COLOR IS RELATIVE TO COLOR AROUND ▮ IT. COLOR LOOKS DIFFERENT IN DIFFERENT ENVIRONMENTS. TO SEE THE COLOR SAMPLE IN ITS "ACTUAL" STATE, EXAMINE IT IN AN ALL WHITE, ALL BLACK, OR ALL MEDIUM GREY ENVIRONMENT. REMEMBER ALSO THAT A HUE APPEARS DIFFERENT IN NATURAL LIGHT, FLUORESCENT LIGHT, INCANDESCENT LIGHT, AND IN SITUATIONS OF PARTIAL ILLUMINATION.

COLOR PREFERENCE · AUDIENCE COLOR PREFERENCES ▮ ARE IN CONSTANT FLUX. THEY VARY ANNUALLY AND SEASONALLY. AGE, ECONOMIC CONDITIONS, SEX, CULTURE, GEOGRAPHY, AND RELIGION INFLUENCE COLOR CHOICES. PREFERENCE TRENDS ARE USUALLY CHARTED AND PREDICTED BY EXPERTS. THEY RECORD COLOR PURCHASES, PERFORM MARKET SURVEYS WITH SPECIFIC PRODUCTS (PAINT, APPLIANCES, CARPETING), DO RETAIL SALES TESTS, AND INTERVIEW DESIGNERS, STYLISTS AND BUYERS. THE COMPOSITE IS ANALYZED FOR PREDICTIONS.

SELECTING COLORS · ANALYZE YOUR TARGET AUDIENCE. ▮ PICK STIMULATING COLORS, THOSE THAT WILL EVOKE A RESPONSE. CHOOSE HUES THAT ARE NAMABLE, WITH GOOD RECOGNITION, RETENTION, RECALL. LIMIT YOUR COLOR COMBINATIONS TO TWO OR THREE. EACH GRAPHIC PIECE SHOULD BE OBVIOUSLY A "BLUE POSTER" OR A "BLACK AND YELLOW" PACKAGE. TARGET SEX, INCOME, AGE, GEOGRAPHY, ETC. RELATE COLOR TO PRODUCT OR SERVICE. CHECK LIGHTING SITUATIONS. EXAMINE SURFACE FOR COLOR APPLICATION, GLOSS OR DULL. CONSIDER REPRODUCTION OF THE COLOR BY BLACK AND WHITE PRINTING AND ADJUSTMENTS NECESSARY FOR PROMOTION ON TELEVISION. CHOOSE COLOR TO RELATE LOGICALLY TO THE TOTAL MARKET, COMPETING VISUAL PIECES.
■REMEMBER COLOR IS THE MOST DIRECT PATH TO THE EMOTIONS OF AN AUDIENCE. IN SOME GRAPHIC SITUATIONS LIKE PACKAGING, SIGNS, POSTERS, AND ADVERTISING IT MIGHT BE THE SINGLE MOST IMPORTANT DESIGN ELEMENT. CONSIDER "COKE", "WINDEX", "PEPTO·BISMO", "COORS", "HEINEKIN", "HERTZ".
■SELECT COLOR TO FUNCTION.. NOT BECAUSE YOU "LIKE" IT!

CAMERA-READY

- CAMERA-READY ART IS THE SPECIALLY PREPARED BLACK AND WHITE ART THAT GOES TO A PRINTER FOR REPRODUCTION. THESE VERY PRECISE IMAGES AND TYPE ARE IN A FORM PROPER FOR OFFSET-LITHOGRAPHY, THE DOMINANT PRINTING PROCESS OF THIS TIME; OR LETTERPRESS, OR SCREEN PROCESS, OR FLEXOGRAPHY.

- CAMERA-READY ART GOES DIRECTLY TO THE GRAPHIC ARTS CAMERA FOR THE RESULTING NEGATIVES, FROM WHICH PRINTING PLATES AND THEN THE FINAL PRINTED PIECES ULTIMATELY EMERGE.

- CAMERA-READY ART (ALSO CALLED A LAYOUT OR MECHANICAL) HAS A MAJOR ROLE TO PLAY IN THE DESIGN/PRODUCTION PROCESS. IT IS NOT AN ACT OF DESIGN BUT CARRIES THE DESIGN IN ITS FINAL FORM, MUCH LIKE A BLUEPRINT CARRIES AN ARCHITECT'S FINAL BUILDING IDEA. IT CARRIES PRINTING SPECIFICATIONS TO INDICATE SIZE, COLOR, BINDING, ETC. CAMERA-READY ART MUST BE DONE WITH VERY SHARP IMAGES. PRECISION TECHNIQUES SIMILAR TO THOSE IN DRAFTING ARE NECESSARY, USING SKILLS IN TECHNICAL DRAWING WITH INSTRUMENTS AND MEASURING, CUTTING, AND PASTE-UP. A DEVELOPED SENSE OF EYE-HAND COORDINATION IS NECESSARY. THE MOST EFFECTIVE GRAPHIC DESIGNERS ARE THOSE SKILLED IN THE PREPARATION OF CAMERA-READY ART. MANY NON-DESIGNERS FIND CAREERS WHICH EMPLOY THEIR TALENTS AS SPECIALISTS IN THE PREPARATION OF MECHANICALS. THESE PRODUCTION MANAGERS WORK WITH LARGE DESIGN FIRMS, PRINTERS, ADVERTISING AGENCIES AND CORPORATIONS.

LINE ART · LINE ART IS MADE UP OF BLACK AND WHITE MARKINGS. TYPE, DIAGRAMS, PEN DRAWINGS, BRUSH DRAWING, STIPPLE OR SPATTER DRAWINGS, ZIP-A-TONE DRAWINGS, SCRATCHBOARD OR ROSSBOARD DRAWINGS AND HIGH CONTRAST PHOTOS ARE EXAMPLES. THEY MAY BE PASTED-UP DIRECTLY AS CAMERA-READY IMAGES. THESE LINE ART ITEMS SHOULD BE DENSE BLACK WITH EDGES THAT MATCH THE FINAL EDGE SHARPNESS DESIRED. OTHER COLORS WILL WORK (ESPECIALLY RED), BUT BLACK IS BEST FOR THE NARROW RANGE LITHO FILM USED IN THE GRAPHIC ARTS CAMERA. THE BACKGROUND PAPER THE LINE-ART IS DRAWN OR PRINTED ON SHOULD BE WHITE.

CONTINUOUS TONE ART · BLACK AND WHITE PHOTOGRAPHS ARE MADE UP OF A VARIETY OF TONES OF GREY IN ADDITION TO BLACK AND WHITE. TO REPRODUCE THESE PHOTOGRAPHS, IT IS NECESSARY TO CONVERT THEM TO DOT-PATTERN IMAGES OR HALF TONES. A HALFTONE LOOKS LIKE A CONTINUOUS TONE IMAGE BECAUSE OF THE RESOLVING POWER OF THE HUMAN EYE. THE MORE DOTS THE PHOTO IS BROKEN INTO THE MORE THE HALFTONE APPROACHES THE ORIGINAL PHOTO IN APPEARANCE. A 150 LINE HALFTONE HAS A HIGH QUALITY APPEARANCE AND MIGHT BE USED FOR AN ANNUAL REPORT PHOTO. AN 85 LINE HALFTONE HAS LESS DOT PATTERN DENSITY AND WILL GIVE THE PHOTO A COARSENESS, SOMETIMES SEEN IN NEWSPAPER REPRODUCTION.

NEWSPAPER HALFTONE

MULTI-COLOR ART · COLORS MUST BE BROKEN DOWN INTO BLACK AND WHITE FOR PRINTING. PRE-SEPARATED ART IS DONE WITH CLEAR ACETATE OVERLAY SHEETS. EACH DESIRED COLOR IS PLACED ON ONE OVERLAY SHEET. THE COLOR AREAS ARE USUALLY CUT FROM RUBYLITH OPAQUE FILM. THIS METHOD IS EFFECTIVE WHEN COLOR REGISTRATION IS NOT HAIRLINE TIGHT.

- COLOR PHOTOGRAPHS AND ILLUSTRATIONS MUST ALSO BE BROKEN DOWN INTO BLACK AND WHITE DOT PATTERNS CALLED COLOR SEPARATIONS. OIL PAINTINGS, COLOR PHOTOGRAPHS (C-PRINTS), AND COLOR ILLUSTRATIONS ARE SEPARATED BY A REFLECTION SYSTEM. COLOR SLIDES AND COLOR NEGATIVES ARE SEPARATED BY A TRANSMISSION OR SCAN SYSTEM.

- COLOR PRINTING IS DONE BY MAKING A SEPARATE NEGATIVE AND PLATE FOR EACH NECESSARY COLOR AND INKING THE PAPER WITH EACH COLOR.

DOWN BOARD · BASEBOARD OR SHEET ON WHICH CAMERA·READY ART IS PRESENTED. CAN BE FLEXIBLE BUT RIGID IS BEST. GOOD BOARDS ARE WHITE, MEDIUM WGT. TECHNICAL BOARD, LINE·KOTE, AND 10 PT. KROMEKOTE.

CROP MARKS · PRECISE <u>BLACK LINE</u> SHOWS FINISH EDGE OF PRINTED PIECE. OUTSIDE CORNERS.

LAYOUT LINES · <u>BLUE</u>, NON·REPRO PENCIL FOR ALL WORKING LINES.

BLEED LINES · <u>RED</u>, INDICATES THAT IMAGE CONTINUES OFF SHEET EDGE. EXTENDS ⅛" OUTSIDE THE MARGINS.

FOLD LINES · <u>BLACK DASH</u> LINES (ABOUT ⅛") WHICH INDICATE WHERE TO FOLD PIECE.

REGISTRATION MARKS · <u>BLACK</u>, STICK·ON, USED TO REGISTER OVERLAYS ON MULTICOLOR WORK. USE THREE AS SHOWN.

■ **PAPER STOCK SPECS** ●
BLACK INK LINE, SHOW COMPANY, PAPER, WEIGHT, COLOR, FINISH. ALSO ATTACH SAMPLE.
EXAMPLE · STRATHMORE FONDA COVER 100# BRIAR BROWN, LINEN FINISH

■ **PRINTING SPECIFICATIONS ·** <u>BLACK INK</u> ●
LINE, KEEP ORDER CONSISTENT, PROVIDE PMS MATCHING SYSTEM INK CHIP WITH NUMBER

JOB IDENTITY →	TIGER BROCHURE
UNFOLDED SIZE →	9 X 12
COLORS/SIDES →	2C-25 RED + BLACK
BINDING →	2 FOLDS AS SHOWN
CAMERA CALL·OUT →	SHOOT AT 100%

PANTONE 485

PMS INK CHIP

■ **COVER SHEET**

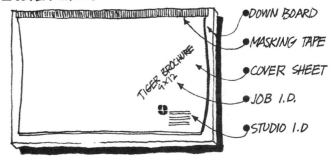

● DOWN BOARD
● MASKING TAPE
● COVER SHEET
● JOB I.D.
● STUDIO I.D

TIGER BROCHURE 9 X 12

WINDOWS · FITTING PHOTOGRAPHS INTO CAMERA·READY ART DEMANDS A SPECIAL TECHNIQUE. PHOTOS NEED TO BE CONVERTED INTO HALFTONES OR COLOR SEPARATIONS, OPERATIONS PERFORMED BY THE PRINTER. THE DESIGNER NEEDS TO DESIGNATE SIZE AND POSITION OF PHOTOS ON THE ART. THIS IS DONE BY CUTTING OR DRAWING AN OPAQUE SHAPE THE EXACT SIZE OF THE PRINTED PHOTO IN POSITION. THE PRINTER THEN MAKES A NEGATIVE FROM THE ART, MAKES A HALFTONE FROM THE PHOTO PRINT PROVIDED, AND STRIPS THE TWO TOGETHER TO MAKE THE PRINTING PLATE.

● CUT SHAPE ON ART   ● PRINTER NEG   ● NEG WITH HALF·TONE STRIPPED IN

● ORIGINAL PHOTO   ● HALF·TONE TO SIZE

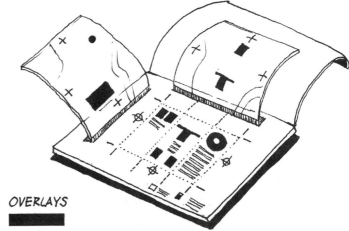

OVERLAYS

THIS SKETCH INDICATES AN OVERLAY TECHNIQUE FOR PRE·SEPARATED MULTI·COLOR ART. THE KEY COLOR, TYPE, AND REGISTRATION MARKS ARE ON THE DOWN BOARD. SHAPES FOR TWO ADDITIONAL COLORS ARE CUT BY HAND WITH AN EXACTO OR SWIVEL KNIFE AND PLACED ON SEPARATE HINGED SHEETS OF CLEAR ACETATE. OVERLAY 'REGISTRATIONS KEY TO BASE BOARD.

GRIDS

GRID · A NETWORK OF UNIFORMLY SPACED HORIZONTAL ▮ AND PERPENDICULAR LINES FOR LOCATING POINTS BY MEANS OF COORDINATES; LINES THAT DEFINE UNIFORM AREAS IN A LAYOUT; A PLAN FOR DESIGNING FORMATS.

MODULE · A STANDARD OR UNIT OF MEASUREMENT; ▮ THE SIZE OF SOME ONE PART TAKEN AS A UNIT OF MEASURE BY WHICH THE PROPORTIONS OF A COMPOSITION ARE REGULATED; REPETITIVE UNITS OF SPACE OR MASS.

SYSTEM · INTERACTING, INTERDEPENDENT, GROUP OF ▮ ITEMS FORMING A UNIFIED WHOLE; A MANNER OF CLASSIFYING, SYMBOLIZING, OR SCHEMATIZING; ORDER FROM ARRANGEMENT.

WHY GRIDS? THERE ARE MANY WAYS TO APPROACH ▮ DESIGN PROBLEMS. NO ONE METHOD IS BEST. GRAPHIC DESIGNERS SHOULD AT LEAST CONSIDER GRIDS AND HAVE AN INTIMATE WORKING KNOWLEDGE OF THEM. THEY WON'T HELP SOLVE EVERY VISUAL PROBLEM BUT OFTEN WILL SUGGEST A RATIONAL APPROACH.

■ GESTALT DATA REVEALS THAT HUMANS TEND TO PREFER ORGANIZED VISUAL AND VERBAL INFORMATION. GRID SYSTEMS ALLOW THE DESIGNER TO SATISFY VIEWER GROUPS WITH RESPECT TO EQUILIBRIUM, SIMILARITY, AND CONTINUATION. THEY HELP THE DESIGNER TO AVOID VISUAL AMBIGUITY.

■ GRID SYSTEMS ARE VALUABLE FOR BUILDING "FAMILY RESEMBLANCE" INTO A SERIES OF VISUAL PIECES. CORPORATIONS WHICH PRODUCE HUNDREDS OR EVEN THOUSANDS OF DIFFERENT PRODUCTS MUST DEAL EFFECTIVELY WITH UNIFIED METHODS OF CATALOGUING AND PROMOTING THEM THROUGH BROCHURES, SALES SHEETS AND ADVERTISING. IBM AND WESTINGHOUSE, UNDER THE GRAPHIC GUIDANCE OF PAUL RAND, HAVE LONG USED GRID SYSTEMS TO BRING ORDER TO THEIR THOUSANDS OF PRINTED PIECES DEVELOPED EACH YEAR. SWISS AND GERMAN GRAPHIC DESIGNERS WITH THEIR DE STIJL/BAUHAUS ROOTS ARE EXPONENTS OF GRID DESIGN. THE JAPANESE, WITH THEIR TATAMI MAT MODULAR BUILDING SYSTEM, HAVE LONG BEEN GRID SENSITIVE. MOST NEWSPAPERS THROUGHOUT THE WORLD HAVE USED GRID-LIKE SYSTEMS TO SPEED LAYOUT AND GIVE A CONSISTENT APPEARANCE.

■ GRID SYSTEMS CAN WORK WELL FOR SINGLE PRINTED PIECES. WHEN AN ABUNDANCE OF VISUAL MATERIAL (PHOTOS, ILLUSTRATIONS, TEXT, HEADS) MUST BE UNITED ON A SINGLE FORMAT, GRID SYSTEMS OFFER A POTENTIAL SOLUTION. ADS, NEWSLETTERS, BROCHURES ANNUAL REPORTS, MAGAZINES, BOOKS, POSTERS, SIGNS AND FILM/TELEVISION GRAPHICS FIT THIS CATEGORY.

■ GRID SYSTEMS CARRY WITHIN THEM THE ORGANIZATION POTENTIAL TO MAKE EXTREMELY COMPLEX INFORMATION UNDERSTANDABLE. LISTS, TABLES, SCHEDULES, FINANCIAL MATERIAL, SCIENTIFIC DATA, AND LEGAL INFORMATION CAN BE MORE EASILY HANDLED BY USING GRIDS.

■ GRID SYSTEMS DO NOT NECESSARILY LEAD TO BORING VISUAL IMAGES AS SOME MIGHT SUGGEST. IF A GRID IS LOGICALLY DESIGNED, AND VISUAL ELEMENTS ARE EXCITING, THEN THE GRID-DERIVED SOLUTION CAN BE EFFECTIVE. GRIDS GIVE YOU A PLACE TO PUT THINGS. THE GRID SOLUTION BUILDS IN ORGANIZATION. VIEWERS SHOULD FEEL COMFORTABLE WITH GRIDS (GESTALT). DESIGN PLACEMENT POSITIONS ARE CUT DOWN DRASTICALLY, SPEEDING LAYOUT TIME. THUMBNAILS COME QUICKER WITH GRIDS. MARGINS, TYPE SIZE, LINESPACING, LINE LENGTH, AND PAGE NUMBERING CAN ALL LOGICALLY DERIVE FROM A CAREFULLY CONCEIVED GRID SYSTEM.

WHAT IS THE GRID? · THE GRID IS A SKELETAL ▮ UNDERSTRUCTURE TO BRING COHESIVENESS TO A VISUAL PIECE. IT'S AN ORGANIZER AND TIMESAVER AND HELPS BUILD CONTINUITY.

● GIVEN A FORMAT SIZE, LAYOUT A SPREAD (TWO OPEN PAGES). ANALYZE INFORMATION PHOTOGRAPHS, HEADS, CAPTIONS, ETC. REQUIRED.

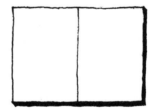

● DESIGN A GRID. APPLY IT TO THE SPREAD. THIS IS A SIX UNIT GRID. IT DETERMINES MARGINS, GUTTERS, ALLEYS, ETC. THIS IS SKELETON FOR LAYOUT.

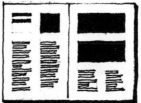

● FINALLY, POSITION ELEMENTS ON THE GRID: HEADLINES, TEXT TYPE, PHOTOS, ETC. THE GRID DEFINES, RELATES, AND SEPARATES VISUAL/VERBAL INFORMATION.

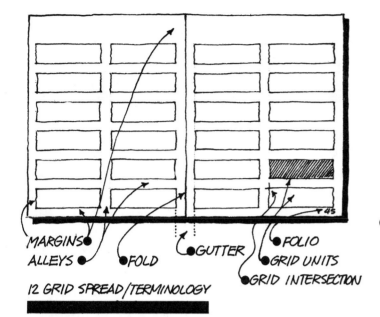

MARGINS●
ALLEYS ● ●FOLD ●GUTTER ●FOLIO
● GRID UNITS
● GRID INTERSECTION

12 GRID SPREAD/TERMINOLOGY

MARGINS • THESE OUTSIDE BOUNDARIES AROUND PAGE
CONTENT CAN BE UNEQUAL IN DIMENSION.
THEY FRAME PAGE OR PANEL CONTENT AND PROVIDE
A VIEWING GROUND FOR IT.

GUTTER • "INSIDE MARGIN", SPACE ON EITHER SIDE
OF THE FOLD. PROVIDES SPACE FOR
BINDING, AND SEPARATES PAGES. ARBITRARY.

ALLEYS • INSIDE HORIZONTAL AND VERTICAL SPACE
CHANNELS WHICH SEPARATE GRID UNITS.
AGAIN, ARBITRARY; THEY HELP SEPARATE HEADS,
TEXT, PHOTOS, AND ILLUSTRATIONS.

GRID UNITS • SPACE MODULES WHICH SET THE BASE
SIZE AND PROPORTIONS FOR PHOTOS,
THE PICA LINE WIDTH FOR TEXT TYPE AND HEADS,
AND RHYTHM FOR THE PANEL OR PAGE.

GRID INTERSECTIONS • WHERE HORIZONTAL AND
VERTICAL LINES CROSS, THEY
CONTROL THE POSITION OF TYPE, PHOTOS, ILLUSTRATIONS.
THEY SERVE AS GUIDELINES FOR PASTE-UP.

FOLIO • PAGE NUMBER AND SOMETIMES VOLUME/DATE
WHICH ARE NEARLY ALWAYS PLACED
CONSISTENTLY (SOMEWHERE) IN THE OUTSIDE
MARGIN.

FOLD • LINE ALONG WHICH THE PAGE IS BOUND.
CENTER OF THE GUTTER, INSIDE
BOUNDARY OF PAGE OR PANEL. INTERRUPTION OF
THE SMOOTH PAGE SURFACE. BE CAREFUL ABOUT
RUNNING TYPE OR IMAGES ACROSS THE FOLD.

NAMING THE GRID • GRIDS ARE LABELED SIMPLY BY
THE NUMBER OF GRID UNITS IN
A PANEL. DON'T CONFUSE THE PANEL WITH THE
SPREAD, WHICH IS TWO PANELS OR PAGES. THE
GRID ON THE LEFT IS A 12 UNIT GRID, BUT THE
SPREAD HAS 24 GRID UNITS.

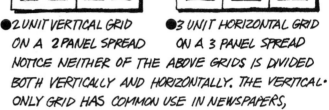

● 2 UNIT VERTICAL GRID   ● 3 UNIT HORIZONTAL GRID
ON A 2 PANEL SPREAD   ON A 3 PANEL SPREAD

NOTICE NEITHER OF THE ABOVE GRIDS IS DIVIDED
BOTH VERTICALLY AND HORIZONTALLY. THE VERTICAL-
ONLY GRID HAS COMMON USE IN NEWSPAPERS,
NEWSLETTERS, BOOKS, AND MAGAZINES.

DESIGNING GRIDS • GRIDS ARE ARBITRARY. DESIGNERS
CONTROL THEM, NOT VICE VERSA.
GRIDS ARE ONLY IMPOSED ON THE DESIGNER WHERE
AN EFFECTIVE LAYOUT SYSTEM IS A TRADITION (AS IN
A NATIONAL MAGAZINE WITH A TRACK RECORD). IN
ALMOST EVERY OTHER INSTANCE IT IS THE DESIGNER'S
ROLE TO CREATE A GRID TO SOLVE THE PROBLEM
AT HAND. GRID DESIGN IS REALLY THE KEY TO
SUCCESSFULLY USING THE GRID SYSTEMS APPROACH.
AN INFINITE NUMBER OF DIFFERENT GRIDS ARE
POSSIBLE, BUT ONLY A FEW WILL PROVE REALLY
EFFECTIVE. HOW DO WE FOCUS ON THOSE THAT
PROMISE SUCCESS?

■ CAREFULLY EXAMINE THE GIVEN VISUAL INFORMATION;
HEADS, TEXT, PHOTOS, ILLUSTRATIONS, GRAPHS, ETC.

■ LOOK FOR SIZE SIMILARITIES WHERE ITEMS CAN BE
GROUPED. FOCUS ON PHOTOS AND ILLUSTRATIONS
RATHER THAN TYPE HEADS AND TEXT. TYPE IS FLEXIBLE!

■ THE SMALLEST PHOTOS OR ILLUSTRATIONS WILL HELP
DEFINE THE GRID. THE KEY IS THE SMALLEST USABLE
GRID UNIT, WHICH BECOMES THE SYSTEM BUILDING BLOCK.

■ DIVIDE YOUR FORMAT INTO GRID MULTIPLES. EACH GRID
UNIT SHOULD BE THE SAME SIZE, SHAPE (USUALLY RECTANGULAR).
SEPARATE THEM WITH ALLEYS, GUTTER.

■ USE DRAFTING INSTRUMENTS FOR PRECISION. MEASURE
EXACTLY IN PICAS. DIVIDERS ARE VERY USEFUL.

■ LAY GRID ON PASTE-UP SURFACE AND PREPARE
CAMERA-READY ART. FOR REPETITIVE GRID USE, INK
THE GRID PRECISELY AND HAVE MULTIPLES PRINTED
IN NON-REPRO BLUE INK.

GRIDS

ABOUT GRID SIZE · A STRONG REASON FOR USING A GRID IS TO PROVIDE PERCEPTUAL ORGANIZATION FOR AN AUDIENCE. WHEN CHOOSING THE NUMBER OF GRID UNITS BEWARE OF TOO MANY OR TOO FEW. DESIGNERS CAN NOT COMMUNICATE EFFECTIVELY ABOVE OR BELOW THE PERCEPTUAL LIMITS OF A VIEWING AUDIENCE. VIEWERS MUST BE ABLE TO DECIPHER A GRID AND SENSE ITS COHERENCE TO BE COMFORTABLE. TWO OR THREE GRIDS PER PANEL ARE TOO FEW MODULES. 72 OR 124 ARE TOO MANY, AS THE AUDIENCE HAS GREAT DIFFICULTY SORTING OUT THE ORGANIZATION. THE MORE GRID MODULES AND INTERSECTIONS, THE MORE LAYOUT POSITIONS EXIST FOR THE DESIGNER. HOWEVER, SMALL GRID UNITS ARE DIFFICULT TO CONSTRUCT, IMPEDE DECISION MAKING AND ARE NOT COMFORTABLE TO THE AUDIENCE. THE GOAL THEN IS TO ADJUST CONTENT TO THE NUMBER OF GRID UNITS WITHIN A ZONE OF PERCEPTUAL ACUITY. CHALLENGE THE AUDIENCE VISUALLY, BUT DON'T COMPLETELY REMOVE CLUES TO THE GRID.

USING GRIDS · IT IS IMPORTANT TO UNDERSTAND THAT EVEN THE WELL-CONCEIVED GRID, ACCURRATELY DRAFTED, WILL NOT INSURE EFFECTIVE DESIGN. THE GRID CAN ONLY PROVIDE LOGICAL POSITIONS FOR PLACING VISUAL MATERIAL, NOTHING MORE. DESIGNERS MUST USE THE GRID CREATIVELY TO MAXIMIZE COMMUNICATIONS POTENTIAL. "WHERE SHOULD I PUT IT?" IS A QUESTION THAT GRIDS CAN HELP ANSWER.

WHERE TO PLACE GRAPHICS · GENERALLY, KEEP CONTENT INSIDE THE GRID UNITS AND OUT OF THE MARGINS, GUTTER AND ALLEYS. THESE SKETCHES SHOW FULL-EMPTY ZONES.

 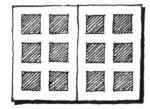

■ ALTHOUGH THESE GRIDS ARE VERY SIMPLE, THE INHERENT ORGANIZATION IS OBVIOUS. THE GRIDS ARE TOTALLY FILLED AND WE PICK UP THE PATTERN AND RHYTHM OF THE REPETITIVE MODULES. NOTICE HOW EACH GRID UNIT IS TOTALLY FULL, NOT PARTIALLY USED. OR HALF EMPTY.

■ USING THE IDENTICAL 6 UNIT GRID, NOTICE SOME SIMPLE VARIATIONS. PHOTOS EXPAND TO FILL 2 AND 3 UNIT HORIZONTAL GRIDS. THE LARGE PHOTO EXPANDS TO FILL 4 COMPLETE UNITS. NOTICE HOW THESE PHOTOS EXTEND ACROSS ALLEYS. ONE GRID IN THE LEFT-HAND SKETCH IS EMPTY. ALL MODULES DO NOT HAVE TO BE FILLED. THE GRID AND ITS VISUAL COHERENCE ARE STILL APPARENT.

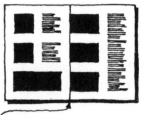 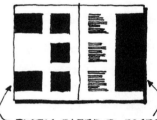

● PHOTOS BUTT TO GUTTER   ● PHOTOS BLEED TO EDGES

■ HERE WE USE THE SAME 6 UNIT GRID AND "BLEED" OR RUN OUR PHOTOS OFF THE EDGE OF THE SHEET. WE ALSO "BUTT" OR RUN OUR PHOTOS TO THE FOLD LINE ACROSS THE GUTTER. SEE HOW THE TEXT TYPE BLOCK CAN ALSO FILL CONSECUTIVE GRIDS BY FLOWING ACROSS ALLEYS.

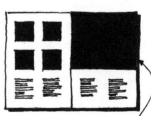 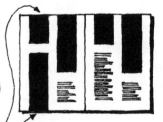

● LARGE PHOTO BUTTS TO GUTTER AND BLEEDS TOP AND RIGHT SIDE   ● PHOTOS BLEED TO TOP AND BOTTOM EDGES

■ ABOVE ARE TWO GREATLY DIFFERENT "LOOKS" USING THE SAME 6 UNIT GRID. BLEEDING AND BUTTING PHOTOS AND ILLUSTRATIONS ARE USEFUL TECHNIQUES FOR ADDING VARIETY TO GRID LAYOUTS, WHILE RETAINING VISUAL ORGANIZATION. REMEMBER, YOU CAN ALSO BLEED A VISUAL IMAGE AND COVER ONE OR TWO ENTIRE PANELS. NOTICE THE TEXT TYPE DOES NOT BLEED OFF THE PAGE, AS THAT MIGHT SERIOUSLY AFFECT CONTENT READABILITY.

ODD SHAPES ON THE GRID · NOT ALL GRAPHIC IMAGES
WHICH MIGHT BE USED
ON THE GRID ARE RECTANGULAR. GEOMETRIC SHAPES
AND THE IRREGULAR SHAPES OF ILLUSTRATIONS AND
SILHOUETTE PHOTOS POSE SPECIAL PROBLEMS.

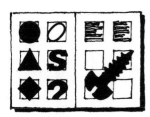
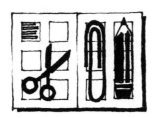

■THESE SKETCHES SHOW OBJECTS OF NON·RECTANGULAR
SHAPES SUPERIMPOSED ON THE 6 UNIT GRID. OFTEN
THE OBJECT NEEDS TO "HANG" OVER THE EDGE OF
THE GRID UNIT TO APPEAR TO FILL IT. THE PICTORIAL
MAY CONSUME ONE OR MORE UNITS, OR EVEN BLEED
OFF THE PAGE.

■DOTTED LINES SHOW
THE GRID IN EACH
SITUATION. THE
UNEVEN SILHOUETTE

SHAPES, SINCE THEY DO NOT FILL ALL OF THE GRID
UNIT, HANG OUT TO COMPENSATE. AS A RULE, POINTED
AND CURVED SHAPES HANG OUT, WHILE CORNERS
OF THE IMAGE SNUG THE GRIDLINE. THE OUTLINE
SHAPES OF AN IMAGE SHOULD CONTACT THE GRID
AT A MAXIMUM NUMBER OF POINTS.

■HERE A SILHOUETTE
PHOTO WORKS AS
THE VISUAL SUBJECT
LAID OVER A 16 UNIT
GRID. (COULD BE AN
AD, POSTER, OR SALES
SHEET). NOTE THE
IMAGE BLEEDS OFF
THE SHEET. THE
TYPE HEAD HANGS
OUTSIDE THE GRIDS.

APPLYING TYPE TO THE GRID

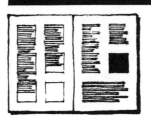

TYPE LINE LENGTH IS MEASURED
IN PICAS, SAME AS THE GRIDS.
THE LONGEST LINE OF TYPE
SHOULD ALWAYS BE EXACTLY AS
LONG AS THE GRID WIDTH. TYPE
MAY HORIZONTALLY SPAN ONE,
TWO, OR MORE GRIDS... BUT ALWAYS ENTIRE GRIDS...
NEVER 1½ GRIDS OR 2¼ GRIDS. VERTICALLY IT IS BEST FOR
TYPE TO SPAN AN EVEN NUMBER OF GRIDS. IF YOUR
INFORMATION IS SHORTER, TRY TO FILL MORE THAN ½
OF THE PARTIALLY FILLED GRIDS. TYPE SHOULD NEVER
EXTEND BEYOND THE GRIDS, EITHER HORIZONTALLY OR
VERTICALLY.

●PANEL
●GRID UNIT
■THIS SKETCH SHOWS HOW
TYPE IS LAID ON THE GRID.
NOTICE HOW THE TOP OF
THE CAPS ALIGN EXACTLY
WITH THE GRID LINE. LEFT
MARGIN WORKS IN THE SAME WAY, BUT INCLINED OR
CURVED LETTERS "HANG." IF ALIGNMENT IS BOTTOM
LEFT, THE BASELINE IS RIGHT ON THE GRID LINE.

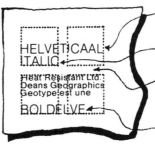

●HEADLINE SPANS TWO
COMPLETE GRIDS
●HEADLINE SPANS ONE GRID

●ALLEY NATURALLY SEPARATES
HEAD AND TEXT TYPE

●HEADLINE SPANS 1½ GRIDS

■THE BEST HEADLINES SPAN COMPLETE GRIDS. THIS IS
USUALLY NOT A PROBLEM BECAUSE TYPE CAN BE EASILY
ENLARGED OR REDUCED. IT IS BETTER TO SPAN MORE
THAN ½ OF ANY PARTIALLY FILLED GRID.

●INCORRECT LINESPACING
SPREADS THE HEADLINE

●CORRECT LINESPACING
KEEPS THE HEADLINE
TOGETHER AND COHERENT.

THE GRID SHOULD NOT
OVERRIDE NATURAL
LINESPACING WHEN POSITIONING A HEADLINE.

GRIDS

TYPE AS THE BUILDING BLOCK · CONSIDER TEXT TYPE [____] AS THE BUILDING BLOCK OF THE GRID. PHOTOGRAPHS, ILLUSTRATIONS AND HEADLINES ARE EASILY CHANGED IN SIZE. BODY TYPE IS GOVERNED BY READABILITY. SIZES SMALLER THAN 8 POINT CAUSE REAL DIFFICULTY.

COLUMN WIDTH · LINES WITH A LENGTH OF 10-12 WORDS [____] ARE THE MOST READABLE. SHORTER LINES ARE ALSO EFFECTIVE. EXTREMELY LONG LINES RETARD READABILITY.

COLUMN LENGTH · DECIDE COLUMN LENGTH FROM [____] MARGIN REQUIREMENTS. IT SHOULD BE AN EXACT NUMBER OF LINES. CAP HEIGHT OF THE FIRST LINE WILL DETERMINE THE TOP OF THE COLUMN. BASE LINE OF THE LAST LINE WILL DETERMINE THE BOTTOM OF THE COLUMN. TYPE DENSITY (GRAYNESS) RELATES TO TYPEFACE AND DEGREE OF LINESPACING.

TOP OF COLUMN●

DASH LINES INDICATE LINES OF TYPE WHICH CAN EITHER CONTINUE ACROSS THE GRID VERTICALLY OR DROP OUT.

BOTTOM OF COLUMN●

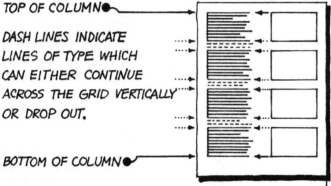

●TOP OF CAP HEIGHT IS TOP OF COLUMN

●ALLEY SHOWING LINE POSITION

●ALLEY SHOWING LINE REMOVED

●BASE LINE OF LAST LINE IN COLUMN

TWENTY LINE COLUMN LAID OVER THREE GRID PANEL

MARGIN VARIATION · EXPERIMENT WITH MARGINS TO [____] ALTER THE LOOK OF YOUR GRID LAYOUT. REMEMBER THAT MARGINS ARE ARBITRARY. UNEQUAL MARGINS OFFER GREAT DESIGN POTENTIAL AS DO UNUSUALLY WIDE MARGINS. BLEED THE GRID OR BUTT IT TO AN EDGE FOR IMPACT.

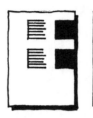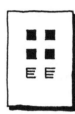

THESE PAGES OR PANELS HINT AT SOME LAYOUT GRID POSSIBILITIES WHEN YOU EXAGGERATE MARGINS.

DENSITY ON THE GRID · BE AWARE OF COMPOSITION [____] DENSITY WHEN APPLYING ELEMENTS TO THE GRID. PAGES WITH ALL GRIDS FULL ARE DENSE AND TEND TO LOOK GENERIC. FILL FEW GRIDS TO GET AN OPEN AIRY APPEARANCE. USE THE UNFILLED SPACES STRATEGICALLY TO AID EYE FLOW.

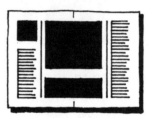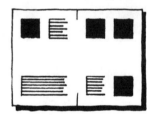

ALL GRIDS FULL   TWO THIRDS FULL

FUNCTIONAL RULES · RULES, LINES, AND BARS ARE [____] OFTEN USED FOR EMPHASIS AND TO SEPARATE ELEMENTS IN GRID LAYOUTS. BARS POSITION INSIDE THE GRID MUCH LIKE HEADLINE TYPE. RULES WORK EITHER INSIDE THE GRID OR WITHIN ALLEYS DESIGNED TO ACCOMMODATE THEM.

MIXED GRIDS · SOME NEWSPAPERS, NEWSLETTERS, [____] POSTERS, AND TECHNICAL SHEETS USE PLURAL GRIDS ON THE SAME SURFACE.

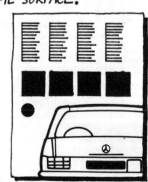

THE INCLINED GRID • ANGLED GRIDS OFFER RELIEF FROM THE FAMILIAR ORIENTATION OF INFORMATION. ALTHOUGH COMPLEX, THEY ARE WORTH TRYING.

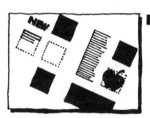

■ THIS SKETCH SHOWS THE LAYOUT FOR A 6 UNIT INCLINED GRID. THE LAYOUT IS MADE ON TRACING PAPER OR CLEAR ACETATE, THEN ROTATED AT THE DESIRED ANGLE. GRID CORNERS ARE TRANSFERRED WITH A PIN POINT, THEN CONNECTED BY DRAFTING. USE A LIGHT TABLE OR YOUR WINDOW TO AID REGISTRATION. TAPE SECURELY.

COVER   SPREAD

■ THE INCLINED GRID PUSHES SOME UNITS OFF THE PAGE. DISREGARD THOSE OR USE THEM TO BLEED SELECT PHOTOS. DESIGN THE INCLINED GRID WITHOUT THE NORMAL GUTTER, AS FOLDING WILL NOT PARALLEL INFORMATION ON THE PAGE.

■ KEEP THE ANGLE OF INCLINATION CONSISTENT FROM COVER TO SPREAD. INFORMATION READING ON AN UPWARD TILT IS PERCEIVED MORE POSITIVELY THAN THAT TILTING DOWNWARD. THE INCLINED GRID IS MORE EFFECTIVE FOR SIMPLE POSTERS, FLYERS, AND BROCHURES THAN FOR LONGER ANNUAL REPORTS, MAGAZINES, OR BOOKS. INCLINED LAYOUTS HAVE DYNAMIC POTENTIAL. SPACES ON THE PAGE TEND TO BE UNEQUAL IN VOLUME. INCLINE HELPS EXAGGERATE ASYMMETRY.

GIANTS OF GRID DESIGN

THIS GROUP OF GRAPHIC DESIGNERS, ARTISTS AND ARCHITECTS HAS HAD SIGNIFICANT IMPACT ON FUNCTIONAL GRID THEORY.

OTL AICHER	ALLEN HURLBURT
FRANK ARISS	LE CORBUSIER
MAX BILL	JOSEP MULLER·BROCKMANN
WILLY FLECKHAUS	PAUL RAND
JAY HAMBIDGE	MASSIMO VIGNELLI

THE INTERRUPTED GRID • AN EFFECTIVE TECHNIQUE FOR ADDING VARIETY TO GRID LAYOUT AND COMPOSITION IS TO INTERRUPT THE GRID. INTERRUPTION MAY BE QUITE SUBTLE OR VERY DRAMATIC. USE INTERRUPTION FOR EMPHASIS OR TO FOCUS ATTENTION ON A SPECIFIC PART OF YOUR LAYOUT.

INTERRUPTED GRAPHIC   INTERRUPTED TYPE

THIS TECHNIQUE IS MOST EFFECTIVE WHEN REPETITIVE ELEMENTS ARE NECESSARY. INTERRUPTION CAN HAPPEN WITH PHOTOS, TEXT TYPE, HEADLINES, OR COLOR BLOCKS. ATTEMPT THIS WHEN YOU FEEL CONFIDENT IN YOUR MASTERY OF THE ORTHODOX GRID.

THE ILLUSTRATIVE GRID ANOTHER APPROACH TO THE USE OF GRIDS INVOLVES GRID IMAGERY AS NON·FUNCTIONAL SUBJECT MATTER. THE GRID BECOMES AN ILLUSTRATIVE ELEMENT RATHER THAN A FUNCTIONAL SKELETON. THE GRID BECOMES VISIBLE AND CONVEYS THE STRUCTURE OF ITSELF. A STRONG ASSOCIATION WITH PLANNING, BUILDING, TECHNOLOGY, ARCHITECTURE AND SCIENCE IS IMPLIED. THE ILLUSTRATIVE GRID IS BEST HANDLED BY EXPERIENCED DESIGNERS THOROUGHLY GROUNDED IN FUNCTIONAL GRIDS.

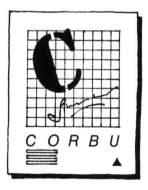
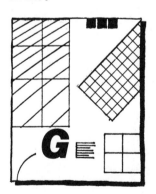

NOTICE HOW THESE GRID APPLICATIONS ARE USED AS DESIGN ELEMENTS. POSITION OF THE GRIDS IS DETERMINED BY THE DESIGNER'S SENSE OF PICTORIAL SPACE. STRUCTURE IS INCIDENTAL. ELEMENTS ARE PLACED INTUITIVELY. WHEN YOU DEVELOP EXPERIENCE WITH GRIDS, THE DIFFERENCE BETWEEN FUNCTIONAL AND ILLUSTRATIVE APPLICATIONS BECOMES OBVIOUS.

PORTFOLIO

port·fo·li·o (pôrt-fō′li-ō′, pōrt-fōl′yō), *n.* [*pl.* PORTFO-LIOS (-ōz′, -yōz′)], [earlier *porto folio* < It. *portafoglio* < *portare* (L. *portare*), to carry + *foglio* (L. *folium*), a leaf], 1. a flat, portable case, usually of leather, for carrying loose sheets of paper, manuscripts, drawings, etc.; brief case.

- DESIGN POSITIONS ARE BASED ON EDUCATION, EXPERIENCE AND PARTICULARLY PORTFOLIO. A PORTFOLIO SHOULD DEMONSTRATE CREATIVE ABILITY, TECHNICAL PROFICIENCY, AND AN ABUNDANCE OF IDEAS. IT SHOULD BE A SYSTEMATIC PACKAGE OF CURRENT VISUAL SOLUTIONS PRESENTED IN A PROFESSIONAL MANNER. DESIGNERS SHOULD AT ALL TIMES HAVE AN UP-TO-DATE PORTFOLIO TOGETHER FOR ADMISSION TO A SCHOOL OR CLASS, TO SHOW A POTENTIAL EMPLOYER OR TO PRESENT TO A CLIENT. SUPPORTING THE PORTFOLIO SHOULD BE A RESUME AND BUSINESS SYSTEM FOR CONTACTS AND APPOINTMENTS.

- MOST EXPERTS AGREE THAT THE PORTFOLIO SHOULD HAVE BETWEEN 10 AND 20 PIECES. CONTENTS MAY BE 4X5 TRANSPARENCIES, COLOR PRINTS, PRINTED PIECES, OR HIGH QUALITY COMPREHENSIVES, (COLOR KEYS, PMT STATS, PHOTOGRAPHS). BEST SIZES ARE 8½X11, 11X17, AND 18X24. THE PORTFOLIO SHOULD BE NEATLY AND SECURELY PACKAGED.

SKILLS EMPLOYERS SEEK

- ABILITY TO EXECUTE CLEAN, NEAT, PRECISE WORK.
- HIGH DEGREE OF HAND-EYE COORDINATION.
- UNDERSTANDING OF PRINTING, TELEVISION, HOW TO ASSEMBLE A JOB, MARK IT UP FOR REPRODUCTION.
- UNDERSTANDING OF TYPE, HOW TO USE, SPECIFY, BUY IT.
- ABILITY TO MAKE ENLARGEMENTS, REDUCTIONS, (VISUALIZER, SCALEMETER, PMT STATS).
- ABILITY TO DO THUMBNAILS AND ROUGHS.
- ABILITY TO CLEAN UP, RETOUCH A SURFACE.
- KNOWLEDGE OF PERCENTAGE SCREENS, HOW TO SPEC.
- ABILITY TO RENDER IN VARIOUS STYLES AND MEDIA.
- UNDERSTANDING OF INK SYSTEMS.
- KNOWLEDGE OF PAPERS, HOW TO SPEC.
- KNOWLEDGE OF PRODUCTION BIDS.
- UNDERSTANDING OF CLIENT COMMUNICATION.
- KNOWLEDGE OF MODEL-MAKING METHODS, MATERIALS.

PORTFOLIO CHECK · DOES THE PORTFOLIO REFLECT YOUR BEST WORK? HAS IT BEEN THOUGHT OUT AND TESTED? DOES IT COMMUNICATE AS A SYSTEM? IS YOUR CRAFTSMANSHIP IMPECCABLE? ARE YOUR PERSONAL STRENGTHS APPARENT? IS THE PORTFOLIO FLEXIBLE ENOUGH FOR A VARIETY OF EMPLOYERS? DOES IT SHOW YOU CAN PERFORM, IMPROVE AND GROW?

SOME CASE/FORMAT/PACKAGE IDEAS

- EASEL TYPE WITH ACETATE PAGES.

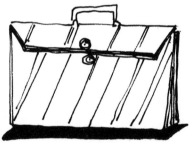

- INTERIM TYPE/CLOTH OR PAPERBOARD/SEMI RIGID.

- ATTACHÉ TYPE/LOCKING/LEATHER· VINYL COVER/FOAM RUBBER PRESSURE PADS.

- BOOK TYPE WITH PRINTED WORK AND STATS BOUND INTO PUBLICATION FORMAT.

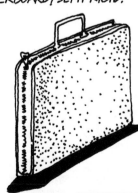

- ZIPPER TYPE WITH PEBBLE BOARD OR CLOTH SIDE WALLS· SEMI RIGID.

- LIGHT BOX TYPE WITH BUILT-IN LIGHT SOURCE FOR VIEWING 4X5 OR 5X7 TRANSPARENCIES.

RESUME

ré·su·mé (rā′zoo-mā′, rez′yoo-mā′, rez′o͞o-mā′), *n.*
[Fr., pp. of *résumer*; see RESUME], a summing up; summary.

MOST DESIGNERS ASSEMBLE MANY RESUMES DURING THE LENGTH OF A CAREER. THE FIRST MIGHT BE FOR A SUMMER JOB OR AN INTERN POSITION. LATER, WHEN SEEKING A FULL·TIME ENTRY POSITION, THE RESUME BECOMES A CRITICAL PART OF THE JOB SEARCH PACKAGE. WHEN CHANGING POSITIONS AN UPDATED RESUME BECOMES NECESSARY. ALONG WITH A CURRENT PORTFOLIO THE RESUME PRESENTS TO AN EMPLOYER OR CLIENT THE HIGHLIGHTS OF YOUR CREATIVE EXPERIENCE AND POTENTIAL. UNLIKE THE PORTFOLIO, THE RESUME IS LEFT WITH THE POTENTIAL EMPLOYER AND BECOMES A PERMANENT FILED REFERENCE. AS SUCH GREAT CARE SHOULD BE TAKEN TO MAKE THE RESUME A POSITIVE, FLAWLESS DOCUMENT.

RESUME CONTENTS· EXPERTS DISAGREE ON THE CONTENTS OF THE RESUME. INFORMATION THAT FUNCTIONS WELL FOR A COPYWRITER IS NOT EFFECTIVE FOR A PRODUCTION MANAGER. CONTENT SUITED FOR A PHOTOGRAPHER SELDOM WORKS FOR AN ART DIRECTOR. A GOOD CONCEPT IS TO LIST ALL <u>IMPORTANT</u> INFORMATION <u>BRIEFLY.</u> BE A TOUGH EDITOR... OR GET ONE! GRAMMAR AND STYLE MUST BE FLAWLESS! CRITICAL DATA TEND TO FALL INTO FOUR DISTINCT CATEGORIES.

- **<u>PERSONAL</u>·** NAME, ADDRESS, TELEPHONE. CONSIDER BIRTH DATE, MARITAL STATUS, HEALTH.

- **<u>EDUCATION</u>·** ARRANGE IN SEQUENCE LATEST TO EARLIEST. FORGET HIGH SCHOOL. PERHAPS GIVE COMMUNITY COLLEGE BRIEF MENTION (A.A.). MENTION CRITICAL COURSES IN ORDER OF YOUR WORK PREFERENCE. IF YOU FILLED AN EDITOR OR ART DIRECTOR POSITION, LIST IT. WORKSHOPS, SEMINARS, AND TRAVEL/STUDY MIGHT BE APPROPRIATE. FOR MOST STUDENTS THIS CATEGORY WILL CONTAIN THE BULK OF THE TOTAL RESUME INFORMATION, BUT IT SHOULD BE KEPT COMPACT.

- **<u>EXPERIENCE</u>·** ARRANGE IN SEQUENCE LATEST TO EARLIEST. BE SPECIFIC WITH YOUR JOB FUNCTIONS. BE SURE TO INCLUDE RELEVANT INTERNSHIPS, CO·OP POSITIONS, SUMMER JOBS. IF YOU WORKED AS A SHEEPHERDER OR AS A SODA JERK THINK TWICE ABOUT INCLUDING IT. HOWEVER, RETAIL SALES OR DRAFTSPERSON WOULD BE WORTH LISTING. WHEN YOU MAKE A LISTING IN THIS AREA CONSIDER THAT A REFERENCE PHONE CALL MIGHT BE MADE TO THE PAST EMPLOYER.

- **<u>AWARDS AND MEMBERSHIPS</u>·** BE SURE TO MENTION YOUR INVOLVEMENT IN AN ART DIRECTORS CLUB, STUDENT DESIGN OR PHOTOGRAPHY ORGANIZATION, ACADEMIC HONORARY, OR EVEN A SOCIAL SORORITY/FRATERNITY IF YOU PLAYED A MANAGEMENT ROLE. IF YOU RECEIVED A SIGNIFICANT STIPEND OR SCHOLARSHIP INCLUDE IT HERE.

OPTIONAL ITEMS FOR THE RESUME INCLUDE:
- REFERENCES (NAME, TITLE, TELEPHONE NUMBER) THIS IS ALSO HANDLED BY THE LINE "REFERENCES AVAILABLE UPON REQUEST"
- EMPLOYMENT GOALS (JOB OBJECTIVE)
- DRAFT STATUS (IN TIME OF CONFLICT ONLY)
- TEMPORARY ADDRESS (ONLY WITH PERMANENT ADDRESS)
- PERSONAL INTERESTS (KEEP TO 3 OR 4 AT MOST)

RESUME DESIGN· RESUMES SHOULD BE TREATED LIKE OTHER PROMOTIONAL PIECES AND DEVELOP THROUGH THUMBNAILS', ROUGHS, AND MOCK·UPS WITH COPY BLOCK INDICATED TYPE. MOST STUDENT RESUMES FIT EASILY ON ONE SIDE OF AN

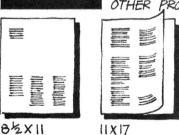

8½ X 11   11 X 17

8½ X 11 SHEET, A VERY GOOD SIZE TO FIT STANDARD FILES, EASY TO MAIL. A STANDARD LETTERHEAD CAN BE DESIGNED TO ROUND OUT THE PACKAGE. THE RESUME CAN BE TYPEWRITTEN OR TYPESET. IT SHOULD BE FLAWLESS MECHANICALLY, DEMONSTRATE A DIRECT DESIGN CONCEPT, EXCELLENT REPRODUCTION, AND WITH ACCURACY SUM UP ITS CREATOR.

SOURCES

■ GRAPHIC DESIGNERS SHOULD BE AWARE OF THE SCOPE OF PUBLICATIONS WHICH DEAL WITH VISUAL COMMUNICATIONS. COMPARED WITH THE OLDER PROFESSIONS SUCH AS ARCHITECTURE, ENGINEERING, OR ART HISTORY, VERY LITTLE HAS BEEN PUBLISHED. MOST RESEARCH RELATIVE TO GRAPHIC DESIGN HAS BEEN DONE BY PSYCHOLOGISTS AND HUMAN FACTORS ENGINEERS. A RATHER UNSCRATCHED MOUNTAIN OF DESIGN HISTORY IS ONLY NOW BEING EXPLORED. CONSIDERABLE MATERIAL IS PUBLISHED ON A PERIODICAL BASIS; HOWEVER, FOR THE MOST PART THIS IS A PICTORIAL RECORD OF THE WORK OF INDIVIDUAL DESIGNERS AND DESIGN STUDIOS.

■ AN UNDERLYING PROBLEM OF TALKING ABOUT VISUAL COMMUNICATIONS IS TRYING TO VERBALIZE VISUAL OBJECTS AND RELATIONSHIPS. MOST OF THE CONTEMPORARY PERIODICALS HAVE BEEN CONTENT TO SHOW PICTURES AND LET THE AUDIENCE MAKE WHAT IT WILL OF THEM.

■ THE FOLLOWING LIST IS NOT DEFINITIVE BUT SHOULD BE USEFUL FOR BEGINNING DESIGNERS. "BEST" LISTS ARE DYNAMIC AND NEED CONSTANT UPDATING. USE PUBLICATIONS TO KEEP ABREAST OF WHAT IS DEVELOPING IN THE FIELD. USE THEM TO HELP STRUCTURE YOUR DESIGN PHILOSOPHY. COMPARE, CONTRAST, GROUP WORKS. TRY TO DISCOVER HISTORICAL FLOW, STYLES, TRENDS, TECHNIQUES, SCHOOLS, AND FORCES.

■ USE PUBLICATIONS BUT DO NOT LET THEM USE YOU. IMITATIVE DESIGN LACKS RELEVANCE AND IS JUST ANOTHER KIND OF POLLUTION!

REFERENCE/ANNUALS

- ■ COMMUNICATION ARTS ANNUAL
- ■ NEW YORK ART DIRECTORS CLUB ANNUAL
- ■ GRAPHIS ANNUAL
- ■ GRAPHIS POSTER ANNUAL
- ■ PRINT ANNUAL CASEBOOKS
- ■ PENROSE ANNUAL · ENGLAND
- ■ CREATIVITY ANNUAL
- ■ SYMBOL SOURCEBOOK · DREYFUSS
- ■ HANDBOOK OF PICTORIAL SYMBOLS · MODLEY
- ■ AMERICAN TRADEMARK DESIGNS · CAPITMAN
- ■ GRAPHIS DIAGRAMS
- ■ MODERN PUBLICITY ANNUAL · ENGLAND

SOME USEFUL DESIGN BOOKS

- ● THOUGHTS ON DESIGN · PAUL RAND
- ● PRIMER OF VISUAL LITERACY · DONDIS
- ● LANGUAGE OF VISION · KEPES
- ● GRAPHIC DESIGN MANUAL · HOFMANN
- ● EXPERIENCE IN VISUAL THINKING · MCKIM
- ● GRAPHIC DESIGN/VISUAL COMMUNICATION · CATALDO
- ● DESIGN YOURSELF · HANKS, BELLISTON, EDWARDS
- ● GRAPHIC ARTIST + DESIGN PROBLEMS · MULLER-BROCKMANN
- ● DESIGNING WITH TYPE · CRAIG
- ● GRAPHIC DESIGN CAREER GUIDE · CRAIG
- ● PHOTOTYPESETTING · CRAIG
- ● LAYOUT · HURLBURT
- ● PUBLICATION DESIGN · HURLBURT
- ● THE GRID · HURLBURT
- ● LIVING BY DESIGN · PENTAGRAM
- ● ASYMMETRIC TYPOGRAPHY · TSCHICHOLD
- ● HOW TO SEE · NELSON
- ● THE DESIGN CONCEPT · HURLBURT
- ● PRINCIPLES OF 2-DIMENSIONAL DESIGN · WONG

PERIODICALS

- ◆ COMMUNICATION ARTS · USA
- ◆ U&LC · USA
- ◆ PRINT · USA
- ◆ INDUSTRIAL DESIGN · USA
- ◆ PUSH PIN GRAPHICS · USA
- ◆ ADVERTISING TECHNIQUES · USA
- ◆ ART DIRECTION · USA
- ◆ DESIGN QUARTERLY · USA
- ◆ IDEA · JAPAN
- ◆ GRAPHIS · SWITZERLAND
- ◆ DESIGN · ENGLAND
- ◆ NOVUM · GERMANY
- ◆ DOMUS · ITALY

OTHERS · DESIGN SOURCES OFTEN BECOME MORE A SEARCH FOR INSPIRATION THAN INFORMATION. SOME VISUAL SOURCES THAT MIGHT TRIGGER IDEAS ARE DICTIONARIES, ENCYCLOPEDIAS, AND EVEN DIRECTORIES.